the
WHOLE
COW

the
WHOLE
COW

Christopher Trotter
with Maggie Ramsay

PAVILION

Contents

the recipes

Prime Beef

Slow Beef

The Often Overlooked

Veal

Introduction

This book celebrates the cow from horn to hoof – I hope that in reading it, you will come to truly appreciate the best of the beast. Cooking for me is more than just providing a meal to be enjoyed either by clients or by friends and family; it's a celebration of who you are and where you are. My cooking is always based on what is available locally and just as important, what is in season locally. In this way, food is always exciting. Shopping in local shops, farmers' markets, and farm shops keeps you in touch with where your food is from and with the people who produce it.

The inspiration for this book has come from my fortunate position of having enjoyed some of the finest beef available, and the desire to understand what it is that makes great beef. My experience as a chef in the Savoy kitchens in London, where hundreds of Scottish beef carcasses were stored in the hotel's cool storage, etched on my mind the importance of source and of aging, as explained later in the book.

It is hard to choose a favourite cut. For both beef and veal, the prime cuts where the meat hasn't worked hard provide the tenderest textures: these are for quick cooking or grilling, sometimes roasting. Really good beef requires very few additions when cooked like this, with perhaps a simple gravy made from the juices or a tangy horseradish or mustard relish. Then there are the tougher cuts, which have been working hard on the animal or are more sinewy because of the part they have played in the animal's life. But these, in turn, provide great flavours when cooked long and at low temperatures. These are often cuts and recipes I associate with winter, comfort food served with mashed potato or polenta.

One must not forget 'the often overlooked'. If an animal must give up its life for our enjoyment, the least we can do is to make sure we use – and enjoy – it all. Do try the wonderful recipes for oxtail and tongue, they are worthy of the grandest of occasions. Veal kidneys with mushrooms and cream take me back to my Savoy days and, for me, calves' liver often has more flavour and melting texture than a fillet steak!

Veal is something I've become a lot more interested in recently and I am delighted to be part of a movement to encourage consumers to eat more veal. I believe that if we drink milk then we should eat veal because it is a by-product of the dairy industry. Male dairy calves provide rose veal and usually live longer than a lamb. Ruby veal is beef cattle bred specifically for slaughtering young. Both provide tender meat with a distinctive flavour. Read all about the veal deal and the history of both beef and veal woven between the recipes – now that really will make a culinary adventure.

After all is said and done, we are what we eat, so take time to choose your ingredients and go for quality over quantity. And remember, sitting around a table together sharing food and conviviality is one of those things that makes us all human, so enjoy!

A potted history

Huge beasts with long curving horns, aurochs – wild oxen (*Bos primigenius*) – were among the creatures hunted by prehistoric man; along with bison, deer and horses, they are depicted thundering across the walls of the caves at Lascaux in South-West France. Until their chance discovery in 1940, the large, lifelike paintings had remained in darkness since they were made, in around 15,000 BC.

Over the following millennia, as herds of aurochs wandered the forests and grasslands of Europe, the animals adapted to local conditions and almost certainly interbred with domesticated cattle. A combination of hunting, disease and competition with domesticated cattle for feeding ground eventually caused the aurochs to become extinct. The emperor Charlemagne is said to have hunted aurochs 'with gigantic horns' in France in 802. Their gradual decline finally ended in Poland, where the last known aurochs died in 1627.

The domestication of cattle began around 8,000 years ago – several thousand years after the domestication of the more easily controllable sheep, goats and pigs. Rock paintings, possibly 6,000 years old, of nomadic herdsmen with their cattle, have been found at Tassili in Algeria. Not only did they provide a ready source of meat and milk, their hides made leather for clothing, tents and receptacles and their dung was an excellent fuel.

Given their importance to humankind, it is not surprising that we have so many words for the animal and its meat. In parts of Bronze Age Europe, cattle were exchanged as a form of currency; owning cattle meant wealth and power, as it still does in many countries of sub-Saharan Africa. 'Cattle' is derived from 'chattel', meaning possessions other than land.

Although it can refer to the female animal, the word 'cow' is also used as the singular of cattle regardless of sex or age (in the same way as we use the word 'dog' for both male and female canines). 'Cow' is clearly from the Anglo-Saxon word *cu*; less obviously it is also related to the Greek word *bous* and Latin *bos*, which also give us the words 'beef' and 'bovine'. The Anglo-Saxons also called the animal 'neat' and 'ox'; 'bull' is from a Norse word brought by Danish invaders; and French-speaking nobility introduced the word *boef* (beef) in the thirteenth century. The Anglo-Saxon word for calf flesh was replaced by the Old French *vel* or *veel*, derived from the Latin *vitellus* (calf). This was also the source for vellum, calf-skin parchment. The word was first recorded in English in Chaucer's *The Merchant's Tale* (1386): '…and bet [better] than old boef is the tendre vel.'

Young cattle are called 'calves' until they are weaned; females are called 'heifers' until they have their first calf; most male animals are castrated to make them less aggressive – these are called 'steers' or 'bullocks'.

For the great majority of people around the world, cattle have been more valuable alive than dead, as working beasts (pulling ploughs to cultivate grain) or producers of milk, butter and cheese. Nonetheless, beef and veal were enjoyed in ancient civilizations. Reay Tannahill's *Food in History* tells of an inscription found in Mesopotamia dated to around 2500 BC, noting that old oxen were fit only for feeding to dogs. The Biblical book of Proverbs, written in the eastern Mediterranean before the fourth century BC, says: 'Better a dish of vegetables if love go with it than a fat ox eaten in hatred.' A third-century BC Chinese poem refers to 'ribs of the fatted ox cooked tender and succulent.'

Beef, whether roasted, fried, grilled or simmered in a rich sauce, has been the focal point of feasts from ancient Roman times to the present day. Records of the most splendid banquets come, naturally, from the literate wealthy classes and it is harder to surmise the diet of the peasant, but – except when times were hard – ordinary people enjoyed roasted meat on special occasions and festivals.

Advances in agriculture in Europe in the early Middle Ages resulted in the production of more, and more nutritious, food. Towns and cities grew around the markets where food was traded and the town dwellers needed a steady supply of meat. In the cities of France, Germany and England, butchers' shops thrived around the great cattle markets. To get to the markets, large herds of cattle were driven hundreds of miles on foot along wide, well-established 'drove roads'. Once again, cattle became an important form of transportable wealth. On the route from Hungary to the markets of Bavaria, herds of more than 10,000 cattle were not uncommon in the sixteenth century. However, cattle droving was not a medieval invention: the ford, or river crossing, used by Saxon drovers gave the city of Oxford its name. So it could be argued that our taste for beef has shaped history, as well as inspiring cooks throughout the centuries.

People often say of the pig that you can use everything except the squeal: substitute 'moo' for 'squeal' and much the same is true of the cow. Mrs Beeton, in her *Book of Household Management* (1861), wrote of the uses of the ox:

> *'There is hardly a part that does not enter into some of the arts and purposes of civilized life. Of their horns are made combs, knife-handles, boxes, spoons, and drinking cups… Glue is made from their gristles… their skins, when calves, are manufactured into vellum; their blood is the basis of Prussian blue [a pigment used by Watteau, Canaletto and Gainsborough]; their sinews furnish fine and strong threads, used by saddlers… their tallow is made into candles; their flesh is eaten, and the utility of the milk and cream of the cow is well known.'*

The latest health research recommends limiting our intake of red meats, which makes sense in evolutionary terms. If you think about it, our hunter-gatherer ancestors ate meat only when their hunt was successful; the rest of the time they survived on wild fruits, roots, herbs, and fish if they were lucky – dairy produce was not available until cattle were domesticated. Remember, too, that the animals they hunted were free-ranging, grass-eating beasts living totally natural lives. Whether you are buying prime rib, mince or calves' liver, buy the best you can afford and give beef and veal the special place on your table that they deserve.

What's your beef?

When you buy a steak or a piece of beef for roasting, chances are, if you think about it at all, you imagine it comes from a picture-book black-and-white cow. But the black-and-white Holstein is kept primarily for its milk, not its meat. Your beef is more likely to come from a black Angus, a red Hereford, a large white Charolais, or one of the many cross-breeds that have been developed to produce both profit for the farmer and good-quality meat. However, new emphasis on cattle breeds and denominations of origin helps distinguish premium beef. Top-end restaurants and good butchers increasingly name the breed from which their beef originates.

For thousands of years, domestic cattle were multi-purpose beasts, providing milk, meat and leather, and working in the fields. Over the centuries, they evolved particular characteristics according to their habitat. In the bleak north of Scotland, with its long harsh winters, the cattle developed thick shaggy coats and the ability to thrive on sparse, rough grasses. Meanwhile, especially in parts of Italy and France, cattle were used to pull ploughs and carts and grew to a great size, with powerful muscles.

During the late seventeenth century, farmers in several European countries began experimenting with selective breeding, aiming to produce animals that grew quickly, gave plenty of milk, or had other desirable traits. One man is often credited with introducing stockbreeding methods that transformed the quality of British beef cattle. Robert Bakewell (1725–1795), an English agriculturalist, allowed mating only between certain animals – for example, those with the largest hindquarters. By the 1780s, after several generations of cattle, he had created the Dishley Longhorn, renowned for its size and the quality of its beef. Bakewell's methods went on to become standard practice throughout

the world. One of his followers, Charles Colling, created the Shorthorn breed, which became even more popular than the Longhorn: a Shorthorn bull famous for its shape and vast size was exhibited around England and Scotland in 1802–7 as the 'Durham Ox'. To this day an experienced stockman can judge an animal's potential from its shape (skeletal and muscular structure); a wide rear end indicates good beef conformation.

Since the early 1800s, farmers around the world have focused on developing certain characteristics in their livestock. For beef cattle farmers, the goal is efficient conversion of feed to meat. Originally grazing was the least expensive way to feed cattle, and three British breeds – Angus, Hereford and Shorthorn – proved invaluable for their ability to convert grass to beef. They came to dominate beef production around the world.

Longhorn cattle

owned by Sir John Harpur-Crewe, Calke Abbey. Robert Bakewell (1725-1795) of Dishley, Leicestershire, improved the breed.

The Spanish had introduced cattle to Mexico in the 1500s, to provide milk and meat, and these were the ancestors of the iconic Texas Longhorn in the early days of ranching. Unrelated to the English Longhorn, these cattle were hardy but very lean. The rapidly expanding market in the cities of North America after the mid-nineteenth century demanded more tender meat, and the ranchers responded by introducing British breeds and cross-breeding them to improve the quality of the Longhorn beef. In 1878, Mark Twain wrote from Europe how he dreamed of 'a mighty porterhouse steak an inch and a half thick…a township or two of tender, yellowish fat gracing an outlying district of this ample country of beefsteak'.

In Argentina and Australia, the beef industry developed in parallel to that of North America. Argentina's fertile pastures and Australia's vast cattle stations proved ideal for stockbreeding. The invention of refrigerated transport in the late nineteenth century allowed exports to the lucrative markets of North America and Europe.

Despite the dominance of certain breeds, some farmers remained loyal to their traditional cattle, such as Lincoln Reds, Galloways, Devons and Dexters, to name but a few. Smaller farmers found dual-purpose breeds particularly valuable for providing both milk and meat. However, as the beef and dairy industries became more intensive in the 1950s, some of these breeds became increasingly rare.

Although beef and dairy farming are specialized industries, much of the beef we eat comes from dairy herds. Dairy cows need to calve every year to continue producing milk, but the dairy farmer cannot keep increasing the size of his herd. Mating his dairy cows with a beef bull allows the farmer to sell the calves to be raised as beef.

As intensive farming became more important, cross-breeding programmes developed Angus and Herefords that were more efficient at converting grain (rather than grass) to meat. Consumer preferences also changed, leading to a demand for leaner beef. Cattle breeders around the world found that breeds from continental Europe, such as Charolais, Limousin and Blonde d'Aquitaine not only produced leaner beef, they also grew more rapidly to a larger size – resulting in more profit for the farmers. A further development was the introduction of Indian Brahman cattle. Heat-tolerant, hardy and disease-resistant, cross-breeds such as Brangus, Braford and Brahmousin have proved popular, particularly in the hotter climates of northern Australia, South Africa, the southern United States and parts of Central and South America.

Fashions in beef come and go. Some consumers demand leaner beef, others look for meat that's well-marbled with fat, or covered with 'the right type of fat'. Here's a quick look of some of the best-known beef cattle breeds.

Aberdeen Angus was developed from cattle native to the counties of Aberdeenshire and Angus in Scotland. Early breeders achieved great success in agricultural shows in England, Scotland and France and the breed was introduced to the United States and Argentina in the 1870s. They are naturally polled (hornless) and are solid black or red. In the United States these are regarded as two separate breeds, Red Angus and Black Angus. Bizarrely, 'Certified Angus Beef' – marketed as natural beef because the cattle are raised without hormones or antibiotics – need not have any Aberdeen Angus blood, it just needs to be at least 51% black! The well-marbled meat is renowned for its taste, succulence and texture.

While the Angus has been bred for its beef throughout the world for well over a hundred years, the original population of pure-bred traditional Aberdeen Angus is now one of Britain's rarest breeds.

Charolais originated in the area around Charolles in the Burgundy region of France. Legend has it that white cattle were noted in the region as early as 878 and by the seventeenth century they were well known in French markets. Selection developed a breed that, like other cattle of continental Europe, was used for draught, milk and meat. French breeders looked for rapid growth and animals that were large, powerful and heavily muscled. Charolais cattle were exported to Argentina before the First World War and soon afterwards to Mexico. In the late 1950s Charolais was the first Continental breed to be introduced to Britain. They also became a popular breed in the United States, Canada, Australia, New Zealand and elsewhere, with lean, flavoursome beef that is a favourite of chefs.

Chianina is one of the oldest breeds of cattle in existence, with a history dating back more than 2,000 years; they were the models for ancient Roman sculptures. The name comes from the Chiana Valley in central Italy. They are the tallest and heaviest breed of cattle, but are known for their gentle nature. Very distinctive in appearance, with well-defined muscling, their short smooth coats may be white or grey and they have a black nose, tongue, eye area and tail. For most of their history they were primarily used as draught oxen, but are now raised mainly for beef. Italy's famous *bistecca alla fiorentina*, a juicy T-bone steak, is usually produced from Chianina cattle. The breed was introduced into the United States, Canada and Australia in the 1970s, and is very popular in Brazil.

Hereford is instantly recognizable by its red coat and white face. Famed for its richly marbled beef, it is one of the UK's most popular traditional breeds. Established in the United States in 1840, it has influenced beef production throughout the world and is often cited as the reason that South America became famous for its quality beef.

Limousin is thought to be a very old breed, but the golden-red cattle, originally draught animals, were developed to improve the quality of their meat in the 1850s and are often referred to as 'the butchers' animal' in their native France. Not only are they very efficient at converting feed to meat, their carcass yields a high ratio of lean, tender meat to a low proportion of bone and fat. Imported into Britain since the early 1970s, they are now one of the country's most important beef breeds, and are equally popular in many other beef-producing countries.

Longhorn is considered to be England's first pure breed of cattle; its coat may be brindled or in various shades of red-brown with white or cream markings. It is not related to the Texas Longhorn. It declined in popularity for nearly 200 years but was rescued by the Rare Breeds Survival Trust. The quality and deep, complex flavour of the fine-grained meat is widely acclaimed by chefs and food writers and the breed is known for its intramuscular marbling of fat that melts into the meat during cooking, resulting in succulent, tender beef.

Shorthorn originated in north-east England in the late eighteenth century; a bull called Comet was the first bull ever to be sold for 1,000 guineas, in 1810. Since 1958 Beef Shorthorns have been developed as a separate breed to Dairy Shorthorns; their meat is well marbled with fat, to ensure good cooking qualities.

Wagyū is simply the Japanese term for 'Japanese cattle', and refers to several breeds of cattle genetically inclined to extreme marbling. It's said that in their homeland the cattle are massaged and that beer or sake is added to their diet of rice, beans, and rice bran, but it's debatable whether this contributes to the quality of the meat, as Wagyū cattle raised on grass and/or grain are equally renowned for their superbly soft, buttery-rich, intensely flavoured – and very expensive – meat. They are now bred worldwide, most notably in Australia, the United States, Chile and a number of European countries, and may be crossed with other cattle, such as Angus.

The Japanese slice this beef very thinly, then lightly poach it or sear it quickly and serve it with a dipping sauce to cut through the richness of the meat. **Kobe** should refer only to beef from the black Tajima strain of Wagyū cattle, raised in Hyōgo Prefecture, although products labelled Kobe or Kobe-style beef are sold in many countries.

Rare and heritage breeds are enjoying a revival of interest, in reaction to the continual 'improving' by cross-breeding and genetic manipulation. Buying rare-breed beef helps to ensure the survival of the breed by providing a market for the beef. Farmers of rare-breed cattle have very high standards of animal welfare and farm with respect for the animals and the environment.

The old-fashioned breeds are relatively slow to mature, which means that their meat develops more depth of flavour than the early-maturing modern breeds. As the older breeds often carry a reasonable amount of fat, they lost further ground during the fat-war years of the 1970s and 1980s.

Apart from the deeper, richer, 'old-fashioned' flavours, the interest in rare breeds is partly due to increasing awareness of the environment: many of the older breeds thrive on relatively poor grasses and hay in the winter; they don't need grain or soybeans. As they are generally free-range, there are few worries about mad cow disease, which was blamed on the fact that some cattle were fed on the remains of other animals.

In the UK, rare breeds are protected and promoted by the Rare Breeds Survival Trust (www.rbst.org.uk). Similar organizations in other countries include the American Livestock Breeds Conservancy and Rare Breeds Canada.

At the time of writing, Lincoln Red, Gloucester, Shetland and White Park cattle are on the Rare Breeds Survival Trust watchlist. The work of the Trust has gained a reprieve for a number of other breeds, including Longhorn, Belted Galloway and British White. All of these, along with other traditional breeds such as the Devon, Dexter, Sussex and Welsh Black, are well worth seeking out in restaurants and good butchers.

Grass & grain

The flavour and texture of beef are partly due to the breed and age of the animal, but even the finest breeds can produce tough or tasteless meat if not reared with care. Diet affects both the speed at which the animal matures and the quality of the meat. Over the past 50–60 years, the many possibilities in farming and 'finishing' systems have resulted in a great diversity in the quality and price of beef.

Cattle, like sheep, goats and deer, are ruminants. Their digestive system allows them to make good use of grass and hay as a major source of nutrients. In nature, they are not grain eaters. They have four stomach compartments, the first of which is called the rumen: here, plant material is partially digested before being regurgitated into the mouth and re-chewed – 'chewing the cud'. This allows them to digest grass efficiently.

From the earliest domestication of cattle, people have moved their livestock in search of fresh grazing land. The Masai cattle herdsmen of Tanzania and Kenya still lead a semi-nomadic life, and throughout Europe, Scandinavia and Asia people have practiced various systems of transhumance – *trans humus* meaning 'across ground' – the seasonal movement of herds from summer to winter pastures. However, in some societies this was not practical; instead, in late autumn weaker animals were slaughtered for meat rather than attempting to keep them alive through the winter on a meagre diet of dried beans and stems, hay and straw – grains were needed to feed humans and could not be spared for cattle.

The idea of feeding an animal on grain and other foods to fatten it up before killing it has been known since ancient times. According to Biblical texts, thought to have been written about 2,600 years ago, the daily food requirements for King Solomon's palace included 10 fattened oxen, 20 oxen from the pastures and 100 sheep or goats, as well as deer and fattened fowl. In the New Testament, written 600 years later, the parable of the prodigal son refers to the killing of a fattened calf for a celebratory meal.

In the early eighteenth century, British farmers began to grow root vegetables, such as turnips and swedes, to feed their cattle during the winter months. Dutch farmers had already discovered that cattle thrived on oilseed cake (the residue left after the oil had been pressed from rapeseed), and British agriculturalists developed the process for cottonseed and linseed 'cake'. Mixed with hay and grains such as barley and oats, the roots and oilseed cake made an early form of concentrated feed. Now that the problem of keeping cattle well fed over the winter was resolved, the way was clear for Robert Bakewell (see page 13) and others to breed animals specifically to improve the quality of their beef; up to this time, most cattle had been dual-purpose, providing either milk or traction (pulling ploughs and carts) and then meat.

Kenya by Eliane Thiollier (b.1926), depicts herdsmen and their cattle grazing on the land.

Unless winter conditions are extreme, it is perfectly feasible to raise beef cattle entirely on grass. A calf born in spring can spend all summer on lush pasture (which includes a variety of plants, such as clovers and vetches), suckling and grazing alongside its mother. Weaned before winter, it can survive outdoors, especially with supplementary feed of hay, chopped sugar beet and other root vegetables. After another spring and summer feeding on the rich new grasses, it can be slaughtered in its second autumn, at about 18–20 months old.

Ranching, introduced to Mexico by Spanish settlers in the early sixteenth century, was a grass-based system. Huge herds of cattle ranged free over a large area from spring to autumn and were rounded up and brought in to shelter or slaughter in the winter. The system spread to Argentina, Brazil – still two of the world's major beef producers – and other South American countries. Australia's vast cattle stations are also based on natural grasslands. The prairies and Great Plains of North America, extending from Mexico up to Canada, were ideal ranchland; previously grazed by herds of bison, and the hunting ground of Native Americans, the ranches inspired many legends of the Wild West and generations of cowboy films.

Corn (maize) flourished in North America, and farmers in the seventeenth century made good use of it to fatten or 'finish' pigs and, to a lesser extent, cattle ready for slaughter. Toward the end of the nineteenth century,

Mexican cowboys on the great plains, where the cattle ranged freely, in a nineteenth-century painting entitled *Ranchers*.

overgrazing had resulted in the end of the open ranges; the ranches were enclosed and corn became invaluable for finishing cattle: corn produces a high proportion of fat marbling in the meat, which is often equated with tenderness and flavour.

After the Second World War there was a huge global demand for food at prices everyone could afford. Farmers sought to increase yields while reducing production times and minimizing costs. When it came to producing meat, be it beef, pork or poultry, intensive farming seemed to be the way forward.

Beef fattening systems in the EU are divided into two main categories: 'intensive indoor' and 'grass-based systems' (often involving winter shelter). However, within these categories there is a wide range of housing and feeding options, influenced by the choice of diet (partly related to climate zone and environment) and by the different cattle breeds. Some are raised on pasture, with grass silage and/or hay as their winter feed; others are kept indoors for four to six months before slaughter and 'finished' on cereal-based concentrate, with straw as a source of roughage.

Silage is made by storing green vegetation in an airtight silo, sealing it in a polythene-covered clamp or by baling it and wrapping it in polythene; the silage ferments and produces acids that preserve it as a high-quality feed. Concentrated feeds can include cereal grains such as corn (maize), barley and oats, legumes such as peas and soybeans, and various types of oilseed cake, with added vitamins and minerals.

In North America, approximately 80 per cent of beef comes from enormous 'feedlots' or feedyards, also known as concentrated (or confined) animal feeding operations (CAFO). The cattle spend the first part of their lives – as little as four months or as long as 18 months, depending on who's telling you – at pasture. They are then transported to feedlots containing hundreds or thousands of animals, where they are fed on a diet comprising 70–90 per cent grain, along with high-protein soybeans, often with added growth hormones, which help to produce huge amounts of muscle mass quickly. (Cattle farmers in the EU are not allowed to use synthetic growth hormones.) Antibiotics are routinely administered to prevent their livers from failing as a result of their unnatural diet. As a result they gain weight rapidly and after three to six months they are ready for slaughter. Many people – and not just vegetarians – consider feedlots to be as inhumane as raising chickens in battery cages or veal in crates.

Feedlots are increasingly being used in Australia and even Argentina, which for centuries has prided itself on its grass-fed beef.

Nowadays, low-cost meat is usually produced from cattle finished on grain, seed and soy-based feed cakes, which makes beef production more profitable. Modern cattle have been bred to thrive on such a diet. However, the cow's digestive system is designed for grass, with nutrients that are absorbed slowly, allowing a beneficial ratio of unsaturated and saturated fat to develop. Feeding cattle on grain alters this ratio, producing more (unhealthy) saturated fat.

Grass-fed beef not only has a lower percentage of saturated fat, it is also much higher in omega-3 fatty acids and CLA (conjugated linoleic acid) – both of which are often lacking in modern diets, and are thought to reduce the risk of heart disease, cancer and arthritis and improve brain function – as well as in antioxidants such as beta-carotene. As grass-fed animals take longer to mature, their meat is generally considered to have a deeper, richer flavour.

Clearly, grass-fed (also known as pasture-raised) beef is worth seeking out. The terms free-range and organic are less specific about the animals' diet, but free-range animals are not kept in confined spaces; organic beef may come from cattle whose diet includes organic grain. Grass-fed beef is gaining popularity in many countries as consumers become aware of the health advantages for both themselves and the cattle.

From the pasture
to the kitchen

To ensure flavoursome, well-textured beef, cattle slaughter should be as stress-free as possible. Over the centuries it has been observed that when animals are stressed before they are killed, they tend to produce dry, dark meat.

In modern abattoirs conditions are strictly supervised and every effort is made to ensure that the operation is instant and humane. Caring beef farmers ensure that their cattle are taken to a nearby slaughterhouse. Unfortunately, some cattle are transported in confined conditions to a distant abattoir, and this increases their stress.

Beef cattle is usually slaughtered between 12 and 30 months old; since the advent of BSE ('mad cow disease'), European abattoirs need a special license to slaughter older cattle. Generally, grass-fed animals take longer to reach optimum weight than those fed on concentrates or cereals. The average weight at slaughter for prime beef cattle is around 350–450 kg/ 800–1,000 lb, and the prepared carcass weighs just over half that.

Dry-aging is the traditional process in which the carcasses (the hide, head, hooves, tail and inner organs having been removed) are split into two 'sides' and hung in a cool place (around 2°C/36°F) until they are judged ready for sale.

Beef is hung to achieve optimum flavour and tenderness, a process that can take up to a month, or even more. An experienced butcher can judge from the look and feel of the meat when it has been hung for long enough, whether this is in 12 or 35 days.

The rich, meaty flavour of dry-aged beef is partly a result of the action of natural enzymes in the meat, which slowly break down proteins and other compounds. The enzyme activity also tenderizes the meat as the connective tissue is broken down. The aging effect differs for the various muscles – those with more connective tissue age faster.

As the meat hangs, some of its moisture evaporates, which further develops and concentrates the flavour.

Hanging beef is a costly practice. It requires a carefully controlled environment and a skilled butcher, and the longer a piece of beef is hung, the more is lost in moisture and the more trimming it requires. Not to mention the time lost before selling the meat. As a result, dry-aged beef is expensive.

Wet-aging is a cheaper alternative to dry-aging and is now widespread. In the 1960s, the advent of vacuum-packing changed the process of maturing beef. Shortly after slaughter, the chilled meat is butchered and then packed in plastic, the air is removed and the packaging is sealed. The meat can be sold within a week of slaughter. The oxygen-free environment slows down the growth of spoilage bacteria and extends the shelf life. The enzymes that improve flavour and tenderness are, of course, present within the meat and it matures in its own moisture. A slightly sour odour is sometimes present when the package is opened: this is a result of the natural maturation process; it disappears within a few minutes and does not affect the flavour of the meat. The mass market prefers wet-aging, as it is more economical – no moisture is lost from the meat and the process doesn't require the skill of a butcher. However, the beef lacks the intensity of flavour it would get from dry-aging.

How much to buy

As a very rough guide, for each serving you will need 125–250 g/4–9 oz boneless meat or 250–370 g/9–13 oz meat on the bone. However, recipes and appetites vary greatly, and you will also need to think about the style of the dish, its place in your menu and whether you want leftovers.

Choosing beef & veal

The first thing to consider when choosing a piece of beef or veal is how you want to cook it. Meat is muscle. So it stands to reason that hard-working, constantly moving muscles such as the legs, tail and neck of older animals will look and cook very differently to the muscles along the back of young animals. But very often, what you lose in tenderness, you gain in flavour – with the bonus that tougher cuts are usually less expensive, although they take longer to cook. Similarly, the amount of fat varies enormously on different parts of the animal: a lean cut may seem a better buy than a fatty one, but – as long as it is not excessive – the fat can help to keep the meat moist as it cooks. Finally, a boneless or boned and rolled cut is easier to carve, but meat cooked on the bone generally has a better flavour and because bone is a good conductor of heat, the meat will cook more evenly. The information on cuts in the following pages will help you with this initial decision.

Another thing to look for is whether the meat has been traditionally butchered or sawn on a production line. A skilled butcher will cut each carcass according to its individual characteristics. Mass-produced meat, cut so that each piece is identical, is machine-sawn; indiscriminate hacking can sometimes mean the meat loses more of its juices as it cooks.

The colour of raw beef can vary from rosy pink to deep, dark garnet red. Many factors influence the colour: the age, breed and diet of the animal; the time and care taken in hanging the carcass; and the individual cut. Older animals generally have darker meat than young ones; this is not necessarily a bad thing, as the meat from a slow-maturing breed may be dark but will have a rich flavour. Much of the meat sold in supermarkets is wet-aged (see page 23), and is usually pink to bright red. It can never achieve the tenderness and deep flavour of dry-aged beef. Meat that has been hung in the traditional way ('dry-aged') for 3 weeks or so will tend to be deep burgundy in colour and will be firm yet yielding to the touch. It is usually more expensive than wet-aged beef, but the extra cost is worth it because the beef is less likely to shrink during cooking, as well as being tender and full-flavoured.

The fat of grass-fed cattle should be firm and a rich cream to pale yellow colour, thanks to carotene, a pigment in the grass. Animals fed or 'finished' on grain will have paler, creamy-white fat. Look for a good outer covering of fat and fine marbling in joints of beef; these streaks of fat melt during cooking, basting the meat from within, which makes it more succulent and tender.

Minced (ground) beef should be deep red; if it is pink, the fat content is too high, whereas if it is brown, it has been in contact with air too long and is not fresh.

When choosing veal, look for moist, finely grained meat: it should not be wet or flabby. Milk-fed veal is very pale pink, while veal whose diet included solid food will be rosy pink or even light red – depending on the style of farming, the calves eat grains, hay or pasture grasses. Veal with a grey or brown hue is likely to be stale. It can be hard to see, but veal should have a small amount of fat marbling; however, too much fat suggests the calf has been overfed. If you buy veal on the bone, the bones should be pinkish-white, almost translucent.

Obviously, when buying products such as veal and rare breed beef online you will not be able to see the meat before you buy it. However, the suppliers are often specialist farmers – who do not produce enough meat to supply supermarkets – and their meat is of a very good quality.

Storing

Store meat on the lowest shelf in the fridge. Wipe off excess blood and moisture so that it is not sitting in a puddle of liquid and wrap it loosely, allowing some air around it but preventing it from tainting or being tainted by other foods in the fridge. A large piece of meat will keep for up to 5 days, smaller pieces such as steaks for 2–3 days. Minced (ground) beef and veal should be eaten within 2 days, escalopes and offal (variety meats) within 24 hours. Vacuum-packed meat can be stored for longer, but never exceed the use-by date.

Beef can be frozen with little loss of quality for up to 6 months, veal for up to 3 months. Thaw, loosely wrapped, in the fridge. Never let the meat or its juices come into contact with other foods, especially cooked foods. Once cooked, cool as quickly as possible, cover and store in the fridge and eat within 2 days.

BEEF CUTS

It's often said that the most tender cuts of any grazing animal are those furthest from the head and the hooves. The most tender of all is the fillet (tenderloin), which lies under the backbone, while the parts of the animal that do the most physical work, such as the neck and leg muscles, provide tough but tasty cuts that need long, slow, moist cooking.

The butcher first divides the carcass along the backbone, into two 'sides', and then around the girth, into forequarter and hindquarter, but that doesn't tell you much about the cooking qualities. The next division is into 'primal cuts' – the large sections from which steaks and joints are taken. These primal cuts have names that the consumer will recognize, such as brisket, rib and loin. Different countries may have slightly different butchering techniques, and the names of the cuts often vary widely from region to region within a country, but the tough and tender parts of the animal remain the same.

CHEEKS

NECK AND CLOD

CHUCK AND BLADE

SHOULDER

SHIN OR

Here we will focus on the meat from the main muscles. Other parts of the animal, such as liver and tongue, are covered in the section starting on page 167 along with the cheeks, heart and tail. This book is divided into sections that group cuts of meat by cooking method, fast or slow.

Cheeks are round pieces of muscle that are deliciously rich and gelatinous after long slow cooking.

Neck and clod (part of the **chuck** in North America) are tough muscles with a lot of connective tissue. They need very long, moist cooking and are often sold as stewing steak, ready-diced.

Chuck and blade are cut from the **shoulder**: the North American 'chuck' covers a larger area of the animal from which various pot roasts are taken. The meat contains quite a lot of connective tissue, which breaks down during long, slow, moist cooking – for example, in a beef bourguignon or pot roast. It is sold in thick slices (chuck steak or the leaner blade steak), or diced as braising steak, or as minced (ground) beef.

Flat iron steak is sometimes seen in restaurants; it is a top blade steak, cut along the grain, rather than across it, giving a well-marbled steak; best marinated before grilling or frying.

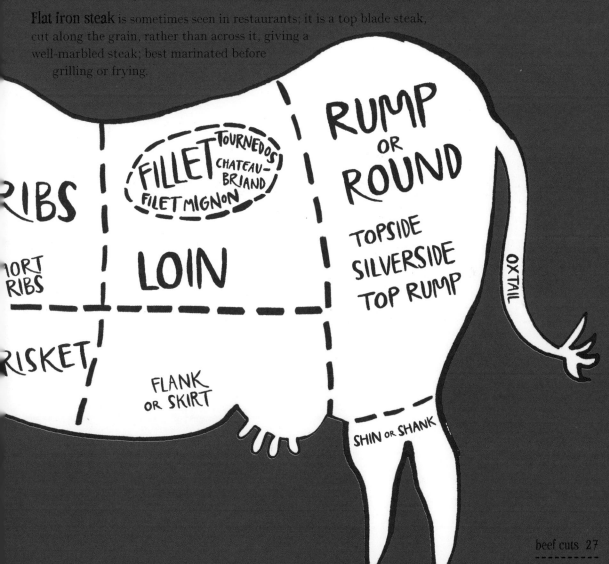

RIBS

SHORT RIBS

BRISKET

FILLET
TOURNEDOS
CHATEAU-BRIAND
FILET MIGNON

LOIN

FLANK
OR SKIRT

RUMP
OR
ROUND

TOPSIDE
SILVERSIDE
TOP RUMP

OXTAIL

SHIN OR SHANK

Ribs are divided into several cuts, which can be cooked on or off the bone. Cut from near the backbone, the **fore rib**, **wing rib** or **prime rib** is a highly prized and very tender, flavoursome cut, interleaved with fat that bastes the meat as it cooks. When roasted on the bone, this is known as a **standing rib roast**; your butcher will happily cut a two- or three-rib piece. An individual rib on the bone is called a **côte de boeuf**; some people consider this the ultimate steak, seared on a hot pan or grill and finished in the oven. The rib can also be boned and rolled as a roasting joint.

Rib-eye steak The meat at the centre of the rib is called the 'rib-eye'. It can be cooked as a whole roasting joint, but is generally cut off the bone and sliced into rib-eye steaks: these are well-marbled with fat and are ideal for quick cooking in a pan or on a hot grill.

Middle rib, between the fore rib and the shoulder, is usually divided into **top rib** and **back rib**. Similar to, but slightly less tender than, the fore rib, they can be roasted or pot-roasted on the bone or boned and rolled.

Back ribs can also mean just the rib bones after the rib eye has been cut away. Popular in the US, they are sold as slabs of several ribs – the meat is found between the rib bones. They are cooked for several hours at a low heat in a lidded barbecue, and the slab is cut into individual ribs to serve.

Short ribs (thin ribs, braising ribs, barbecue ribs, Jacob's ladder), further down toward the breast, have a good covering of meat, well marbled with fat. The bones are usually about 8–12 cm/3–5 in long, and may be sold individually or in a slab. They have lots of flavour, but they need long slow cooking, either braised or in a lidded barbecue; after 2 or 3 hours they become meltingly tender.

Brisket is the breast, sold boned and, usually, rolled. It has a distinctive coarse grain, plenty of connective tissue and can be fatty, but is a very versatile cut. In many countries it is the basis of a boiled beef dinner, in which it is not boiled, but simmered with vegetables for several hours.

Usually cooked as a whole joint, it can be braised or pot-roasted. It is also brined to make corned or salt beef.

Flank means different things to different butchers, and is sometimes used interchangeably with **skirt**. In its broadest sense, flank can mean the whole of the underside of the animal (forequarter and hindquarter flanks). As this is a large area, some flank steak is tough and fatty, best braised, pot-roasted or minced (ground), while other flank steaks are lean enough to be grilled, especially if they are first marinated: excellent for fajitas and kebabs. The American dish **London broil** is based on a piece of marinated flank steak that is quickly grilled (broiled), then sliced across the grain.

French butchers have developed different techniques and created various steaks that are becoming increasingly popular in other countries. **Bavette (skirt steak, flank steak)** taken from the internal part of the rib cage can be cooked quickly over high heat and sliced across the grain. **Onglet (hanger steak, feather steak)** has great flavour and cooks very quickly in a pan, grill or barbecue.

The loin, or **sirloin**, begins where the ribs end. This primal cut provides some of the most highly prized tender cuts, under a whole host of names. It can be roasted whole, or boned and rolled. It is often cut into **sirloin steaks**, on or off the bone, for frying or grilling. It's also ideal for a stir-fry because it cooks quickly and, although expensive, you don't need much.

Porterhouse and **T-bone** steaks are cut across the sirloin, on the bone; the T-bone – Italy's famous *bistecca alla fiorentina* – includes a section of the fillet. Both are cooked quickly over high heat and best served rare.

Fillet (tenderloin, filet mignon, tournedos, chateaubriand), the most tender cut of all, is a long muscle that forms part of the sirloin. It is most often cut into steaks for grilling or frying, but it can be roasted in one piece, sometimes called a chateaubriand. Its quick cooking time makes it ideal for beef Wellington or boeuf en croûte (beef cooked in pastry).

The **rump** is where the loin meets the top of the hind leg. It comprises several different muscles collectively known as rump steak, one of Britain's most popular cuts. Chewier than sirloin, it nonetheless has excellent flavour and is cut into thick slices for grilling, frying or barbecuing over high heat. Larger pieces can be roasted.

The upper hind leg or rear end of the animal is a primal cut known in North America as the **round**. It is subdivided into several smaller cuts. Round cuts are quite tough and generally best suited to long, moist cooking methods.

Topside (top round) is a lean, fine-grained boneless cut from the inside of the leg. In the UK it is usually sold rolled. Suitable for pot-roasting and braising, it can also be roasted, with a piece of barding fat tied around it to baste it and keep it moist as it cooks. **Silverside** is a British cut from the outside of the hind leg, sold fresh or salted, usually rolled. Lean and coarse-grained, it is often used for making boiled beef dishes, braises and pot roasts, and also for spiced beef and corned beef (salt beef). The US cuts known as **bottom round** and **rump roast** are less tender than the top round and are best pot-roasted.

Top rump or **thick flank** is a lean cut from the inside of the upper leg. Similar to topside, but a little more tender, it can be sliced to make inexpensive frying steak. It can also be used for casseroles.

Shin (shank, leg) is one of the toughest cuts; it is ideal for stews and is often sold sliced or diced as stewing steak. The whole joint, off or on the bone, can also be cooked slowly at a low temperature. Some butchers call the front leg shin, or foreshank, while the hind limb is sold as leg – also known as hock or, in Scotland, hough.

Oxtail is bony, fatty, gelatinous – but transformed by long, moist cooking into a delicious and distinctively flavoursome casserole or soup. The tail is usually sold separated into pieces; if you buy a whole tail, ask your butcher to chop it for you.

Minute steak is a small, thinly sliced, boneless steak for quick frying or grilling over high heat. It is best served rare and will become tough if overcooked. It may be from the sirloin, but is more likely to be from the top rump, flank or skirt (*bavette*).

Minced (ground) beef can be made from any part of the animal, and you can't always be sure which part. Minced chuck has a high fat content, which makes juicy hamburgers and meatloaf. Topside (top round), flank and even sirloin provide very lean mince.

VEAL CUTS

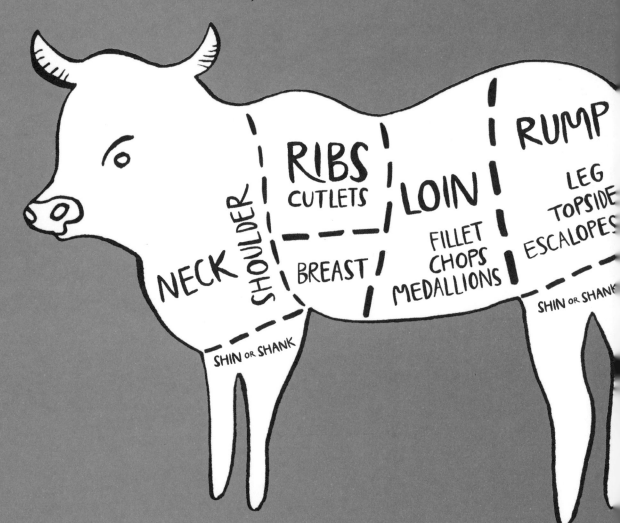

Neck and **shoulder** (sometimes called the **oyster**) are best cooked slowly: braised, pot-roasted or poached, as in blanquette de veau (see page 245). Often sold boned and rolled, or cut into chunks for stews and pies.

Breast has a little more fat than other veal cuts. It can be roasted on the bone, but is often boned, stuffed and rolled (see page 243). The hind part comprises **riblets (short ribs, tendrons)** for grilling, roasting or braising.

Best end of neck is the tender meat of the central **ribs**. Usually sold on the bone for roasting as a **rack of veal (carré de veau)**. Removing the chine bone (backbone) makes carving easier.

Cutlets from the best end of neck can be quickly fried, grilled or barbecued over a high heat.

Loin is very tender and lean and is ideal for roasting, either on the bone or boned and rolled. The **fillet** may be included in a loin joint but is often removed and sold separately as a luxurious roasting joint, or cut into **medallions**, the veal equivalent of fillet steaks.

Chops taken from the loin are the veal equivalent to a beef T-bone steak – best grilled or fried at a high heat.

Rump (top round, quasi) is usually sold boned as a roasting joint.

Leg is a large cut that can be roasted whole or boned and stuffed, but is usually divided into smaller cuts such as **topside (cushion, top round)**, which are often better braised or pot-roasted.

Escalopes are very lean, boneless slices taken from various muscles in the hindquarters, particularly the leg.

Shin (shank), from either the fore or hind leg, is a sinewy cut that needs long, slow, moist cooking, on or off the bone. When sliced across through the bone, you get a cut known as **osso buco**, used for a classic Italian braise (see page 236). The bony hind leg is also known as the **knuckle**; the meat can be stewed and the bone chopped and used to make veal stock.

Stewing veal, usually cut from the neck or shoulder, is best cooked slowly, with stock or wine.

Minced (ground) veal is leaner and more tender than beef mince; ideal for pâtés and terrines, meatballs and veal burgers.

PRIME BEEF

The Steaks

Roasting chunks of meat on a stick held in the fire was probably prehistoric man's first venture in cooking. The roasting spit seems to have been a natural development, and we get our word 'steak' from the Old Norse word *steikja*, which meant 'to roast on a spit'. We no longer cook steaks on a spit, but some of the best, most tender beef still gets its flavour from fire – be it a smoking hot griddle pan, the fierce flame grill of a restaurant, or the glowing coals of a barbecue.

'Steak' can be used for any meat, but in most countries the first thing that comes to mind is an individual cut of beef, seared to give a tasty brown exterior and juicy interior. Names of the cuts vary from country to country and from region to region, some steaks being more instantly recognizable than others.

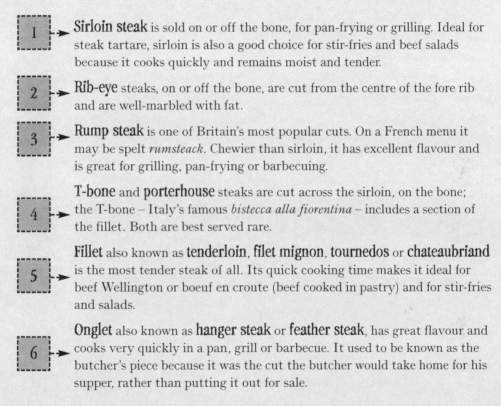

1 Sirloin steak is sold on or off the bone, for pan-frying or grilling. Ideal for steak tartare, sirloin is also a good choice for stir-fries and beef salads because it cooks quickly and remains moist and tender.

2 Rib-eye steaks, on or off the bone, are cut from the centre of the fore rib and are well-marbled with fat.

3 Rump steak is one of Britain's most popular cuts. On a French menu it may be spelt *rumsteack*. Chewier than sirloin, it has excellent flavour and is great for grilling, pan-frying or barbecuing.

4 T-bone and **porterhouse** steaks are cut across the sirloin, on the bone; the T-bone – Italy's famous *bistecca alla fiorentina* – includes a section of the fillet. Both are best served rare.

5 Fillet also known as **tenderloin**, **filet mignon**, **tournedos** or **chateaubriand** is the most tender steak of all. Its quick cooking time makes it ideal for beef Wellington or boeuf en croute (beef cooked in pastry) and for stir-fries and salads.

6 Onglet also known as **hanger steak** or **feather steak**, has great flavour and cooks very quickly in a pan, grill or barbecue. It used to be known as the butcher's piece because it was the cut the butcher would take home for his supper, rather than putting it out for sale.

What's at steak?

Steaks of venison or beef, griddled until brown and served with a sauce of vinegar, verjuice, wine, pepper, ginger and cinnamon – substitute tamarind for verjuice, and you might almost be reading a modern Indonesian recipe. But, in fact, this is one of the earliest known references to 'steak' and it is found in a fifteenth-century manuscript in the British Library.

The tantalizing aroma of cooked beef was one of the temptations of an early fifteenth-century visitor to London. The narrator of the poem 'London Lickpenny' (referring to London 'licking up' money) talks of 'Ribs of beef and many a pie' sold by the city's street vendors, along with mackerel, hot sheep's feet and strawberries.

England's reputation for its beef grew as large numbers of English cattle were raised specifically for eating: the beef would have been more tender than that from old oxen and cows who had outlived their usefulness as working animals and milk providers. The diarist Samuel Pepys, writing on Saturday 11 February 1660, records a spontaneous political celebration in the streets of London; he saw more than fifty bonfires, on which 'rumps tied upon sticks' were being roasted. The beefsteak came to symbolize British liberty and prosperity.

The first beefsteak club was founded in London in 1705, with members active in the arts and politics. Other such clubs appeared in London and other cities, including Dublin and Philadelphia. The most famous and longest-lived club was the Sublime Society of Beef Steaks, founded in 1735, whose motto was 'Beef and Liberty', with a symbol of the gridiron on which the steaks were cooked. The 24 members met regularly and enjoyed their steaks with baked potatoes and onions. Were these the precursors of today's steakhouses?

London's oldest existing restaurant, Rules, opened in 1798 in Maiden Lane in the City of Westminster. Although its menu is not stuck in the past, Rules serves traditional British food, including steaks, roast rib of beef, steak and kidney pies and puddings, and game in season. Rules owns the Lartington Estate in the High Pennines in north-east England, where Belted Galloway beef is farmed to supply the restaurant.

In over four hundred years, England's reputation for fine beef has rarely wavered. Alexandre Dumas, writing his *Grand Dictionnaire de Cuisine* in the mid-nineteenth century, says: 'I remember seeing the birth of beefsteak in France, after the 1815 campaign [the Battle of Waterloo], when the English stayed in Paris for two or three years.' He goes on to describe the cooking method, in a special cast-iron plate, thoroughly heated over live coals, with the beef 'turned only once in order to conserve its juices.' He says that in an English tavern it would be served with anchovy butter but that the best accompaniment for a French beefsteak is maître d'hôtel sauce, made with herbs and lemon.

French cooking became increasingly elaborate during the nineteenth century. One of the most renowned and luxurious of all steak dishes, Tournedos Rossini combines fillet steak with foie gras, truffles and a rich demi-glace sauce. It is named in honour of the Italian composer Gioachino Rossini (1792 1868); he was a renowned gourmet who spent many years in Paris. By the end of the century, chef Auguste Escoffier had worked in some of the finest hotels and restaurants in Europe, including the Ritz in London. His book, *Le Guide Culinaire*, included sixty recipes for tournedos, fifty for filet de boeuf, and recipes for lungs, udder, palates and brains.

However, French country cooking has always been a world away from the cuisine of Paris. In the wine-producing region of Bordeaux, beef steaks are simply grilled over a fire of vine cuttings and topped with a mixture of finely chopped shallots, parsley and bone marrow.

Simplicity is also the key to *churrasco*, the meat – usually beef – grilled over fire that meat lovers dream of when they think about the food of Argentina, Uruguay and southern Brazil. It has been suggested that the word *churrasco* comes from the sound of the fat dripping onto the coals.

MILORD BIFTECK.

Milord Bifteck – the English as seen by the French. A caricature image from Nancy, France, early 19th century.

In a *churrascaria* – a restaurant that specializes in this style of cooking – a large steak or several smaller ones may be threaded onto a skewer before being cooked on a *parilla* (grill). The meat is served with *chimichurri*, a sort of vinaigrette flavoured with garlic, parsley and oregano. Argentina and Brazil vie with the US and Canada as the world's greatest beef-eaters in terms of per capita consumption.

The simple burger has a surprisingly complex history for a modern icon. In German the term Hamburger steak means 'a steak from Hamburg'. Rissoles (derived from the Latin for 'reddish paste') and patties of chopped beef had been prepared in Europe for hundreds of years; it is thought that early nineteenth-century German immigrants arriving in the US from the port of Hamburg brought their own particular recipe for beef patties, which became widely known. A recipe for Hamburg steaks appears in Fannie Farmer's *Boston Cooking School Cook Book* (1896); they are made from finely chopped lean beef, highly seasoned and flavoured with a few drops of onion juice or half a finely chopped shallot. The hamburger in a bun was introduced to a wider audience at the St Louis World's Fair in 1904, and it has since gone global. In France they call it *steak haché* (chopped steak) and it's often served *'à cheval'* – which is nothing to do with horsemeat, it simply means 'with a fried egg on top'.

At first glance a steak tartare may look like a hamburger – and it's often served with thin chips (French fries) – but it's raw! Legends tell of nomadic Tartar horsemen placing a piece of meat under their saddles to tenderize it as they galloped across the Steppe, but leather and horse sweat don't generally make a tasty sauce. The French word *tartare* does refer to these tribes, and in *Food in History* (1988) Reay Tannahill suggests a possible link: when Marco Polo travelled through China in the thirteenth century he found that the people of Yunnan in western China liked to eat raw meat; and when he wrote about his travels he often referred to all Chinese as 'Tartars' – it would be pleasing to think that someone made this connection when naming the dish. However, it first appeared on menus in France's grand hotels at the turn of the twentieth century, with the name *beefsteak à l'Americaine*. It's not clear why the dish was associated with America – perhaps in recognition of the quality of the meat, or maybe as a political gesture. The raw chopped meat was served with a raw egg yolk on top and capers, chopped onion and chopped parsley on the side. In 1921, in a revised edition of his *Guide Culinaire*, Escoffier included a recipe for *beefsteak à la tartare* (without the egg yolk and with *sauce tartare* on the side) as a variation of *beefsteak à l'Americaine*. The Belgians are more likely to call it *filet américain* rather than *boeuf tartare*. The dish became more fashionable after the Second World War.

Beef is the most commonly eaten meat in Korea. Spicy soups, stews and hot-pots make good use of tougher cuts, while the tender sirloin and rib steaks are used in some of Korea's classic dishes, such as *yukhoe*, made with marinated raw beef, like a Korean steak tartare – hmm, maybe the dish really does have a connection with the Tartars. Better known in the West are *bulgogi* ('fire meat') – marinated pieces of steak cooked until sizzling on an iron grill – and stir-fries of meat, noodles and vegetables, such as the popular *chapchae*.

Japan's celebrated Wagyū beef makes deliciously melt-in-the-mouth *sashimi*: a piece of steak seared in a hot pan for a few seconds, then sliced thinly and served with a dipping sauce. Wagyū could also be used in *sukiyaki*, a one-pot dish cooked at the table, in which thinly sliced beef is seared and simmered with tofu, noodles, spring onions and other ingredients – but that would make an expensive *sukiyaki*. It would be very extravagant indeed to use Wagyū for *shabu shabu*, a sort of Japanese beef fondue, where each diner picks up pieces of meat and vegetables with chopsticks and swishes them around in a pot of boiling broth until they are cooked. All are nineteenth- or twentieth-century creations. For more than a thousand years, Japan generally followed the Buddhist path of eating no meat or poultry. In the 1850s, after more than two hundred years of isolation, the country entered a period of industrialization and exchange with the West. Young Japanese intellectuals were particularly keen to embrace the habits of the Europeans and Americans – including eating meat.

The vast and varied cuisines of China, Indonesia and Thailand use beef – indeed all meat – sparingly, but nonetheless have extensive repertoires of slow-cooked braises and curries. All around the world, however, their best-known dishes use tender beef, often marinated for extra flavour and tenderness, and then cooked quickly: stir-fries; satay; sizzling hot grilled beef cooked on a cast-iron grill; and Thailand's beef salad, in which the steak is seared, sliced thinly and served with a hot-sour-sweet dressing and a glorious pile of fresh coriander and mint.

HOW TO COOK A STEAK

Whether it's a tender fillet, a handsome T-bone or a firm rump, any lean beef steak can be savoury and succulent if you follow a few basic principles.

SIZE

It's not so much the weight of the steak but the thickness that matters. It needs to be reasonably thick, otherwise the inside will be overcooked before the outside has formed the delicious crust required for maximum flavour, so make sure it's at least 2 cm/¾ in thick.

The classic fillet steak is round, as it is cut across a single muscle – the tapering fillet end is often slightly less expensive. A piece of rump may be different shapes because it comes from a larger section of the animal. A good butcher may be able to offer you a seam-cut rump, which means you are getting meat from just one piece of muscle.

TENDERNESS AND FLAVOUR

There is a simple rule of thumb: the less work the muscle has to do on the animal, the more tender the meat will be, but also the less flavour it will have. Thus a fillet steak has a lovely buttery tenderness but little flavour. Rump, or one of the increasingly popular French cuts from the skirt such as *bavette* or *onglet*, have great flavour but require a bit more tooth work.

PREPARATION

If you buy a steak in a vacuum pack, remove it from the pack at least 30 minutes before you cook it: it needs to breathe! Contact with oxygen will reawaken the natural flavours of the meat. Never cook a steak – or any meat – straight from the fridge: bring it up to room temperature for 1 hour. You don't want the meat to be cold in the middle. Just before you cook it, make sure the meat is really dry; pat it with kitchen paper to remove any blood or water. This creates the best possible conditions for getting a lovely flavoursome brown crust.

COOKING

Intense heat is required. This also means smoke! So if you are cooking in the kitchen, make sure that either the windows are open or the extractor fan is on, and doors to the rest of the house are closed. If you are cooking outdoors, just enjoy that aromatic, appetizing smoke. Never cook a steak under a domestic grill: the heat simply isn't high enough.

You will need a cast-iron griddle pan or barbecue – which will give you those dark stripes that restaurants produce on a professional flame grill – or a heavy-bottomed frying pan (skillet), in which you can then create a sauce based on the steak cooking juices.

If you are cooking in a heavy frying pan, place it over a medium heat and gradually increase the heat until it is smoking hot. Season the steaks with salt and pepper. Add a tablespoon of oil and a little butter to the pan, then place the steaks firmly in the pan. Brown on one side and then turn and brown on the other. You then need to brown the edges: if this means leaning the steaks against the side of the pan or using a pair of tongs, so be it, but don't jiggle the pan or constantly move the meat. It needs steady, intense heat and minimum movement. Once browned all over, reduce the heat to cook the steak to your liking. This may mean straight out – 'blue' – or maybe 2–3 minutes for rare, 3–4 for medium.

If you want to use the cooking juices as the base for your sauce you may need to wipe the pan with kitchen paper to remove any burnt bits.

If cooking on a barbecue or griddle pan, get them supremely hot. Roll the meat in a little oil before seasoning and then place firmly on the hot surface and cook as above.

RESTING

Once cooked, allow the steak to rest in a warm place (such as the oven, recently turned off) for about 5 minutes – slightly more for rare, slightly less for medium. The heat will continue to permeate the meat for a certain amount of time, and it's a question of balancing the cooking time and resting time, but all steaks need to rest, otherwise the juices will bleed all over the plate and the meat will be tough. At high temperatures the muscle tissue contracts and becomes taut; the resting time allows the muscle to relax and the juices to permeate the whole cut.

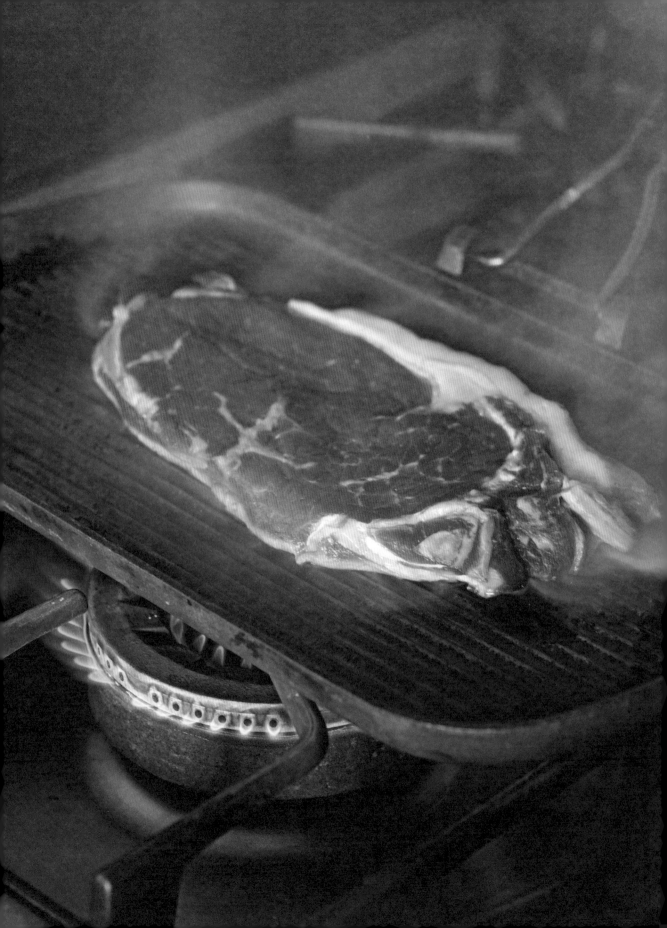

Be brave! Get the griddle pan smoking hot before cooking your steak on it.

Steak au poivre

Nothing fancy – but I like the crunch and fiery heat of the peppercorns contrasting with the rich creamy sauce. I always use black peppercorns: I have never liked white ones because I find their flavour somewhat acrid, but by all means use pink or green peppercorns.

SERVES 4

2–3 tbsp black
  peppercorns
4 rump steaks
1 tbsp olive oil
25 g/1 oz/2 tbsp butter
1 tbsp whisky
125 ml/4 fl oz/½ cup stock
100 ml/3½ fl oz/6–7 tbsp
  double (heavy) cream
salt

Coarsely crush the peppercorns. You can use a pestle and mortar; I undo the top of my pepper mill so it's just loosely attached, and this gives a coarse grind. Some mills have different levels of grinding, but it's important not to grind the pepper too finely because this makes the sauce too peppery-hot. Press the steaks into the crushed peppercorns and coat them all over.

Get a heavy frying pan (skillet) very hot. Add the oil, then add the steaks, pressing them down with a spatula, and cook to form a good crust, carefully turning them with tongs to get a crust all over. Reduce the heat, add the butter and spoon it over the steaks until done to your liking. Remove from the pan and leave to rest in a warm place.

Add the whisky and once it has bubbled up, add the stock and boil to reduce by half. Add the cream and reduce to a pouring sauce. Season with salt to taste, pour over the steaks and serve immediately.

Bavette aux échalotes

My version of a French bistro classic. The French have long appreciated skirt steak (*bavette*); it needs to be carefully trimmed, but good butchers will do this before they put the meat out for sale. It needs to be served rare — if overcooked, it can become tough. Traditionally served with thin, crisp chips, it's also very good with quickly cooked greens such as kale or sprout tops.

SERVES 4

55 g/2 oz/4 tbsp cold
   butter, cubed
8 shallots, peeled
125 ml/4 fl oz/^{1}/$_2$ cup
   red wine
4 skirt (*bavette*) steaks
   (200/7 oz each and 2–3
   cm/about 1 in thick)
salt and pepper
a little olive oil
a sprig of thyme

In a small pan, heat half the butter and cook the shallots gently until golden brown but not too soft. Set aside and add the red wine to the juices in the pan.

Prepare the steaks (see pages 42–43) and cook in a little oil and butter in a very hot, heavy frying pan (skillet) over a high heat for just 2 minutes on each side. Remove from the pan and leave in a warm place to rest.

Reduce the heat and add the shallots and wine, along with the thyme, and boil to reduce to about 2 tablespoons: the shallots should offer a little resistance if pierced with a sharp knife. Remove from the heat, remove the thyme, swirl in the remaining cold butter and season to taste. Slice each steak across the grain into four or five slices and serve immediately.

Tournedos Rossini

I can't resist this glorious representation of that bygone world of the great kitchen. When I started my training at the Savoy in London there were 100 cooks in the kitchen. Everything was prepared by hand. Soups were passed through sieves because we had no food processors. The repertoire of steak 'garnishes' was huge, but Rossini had it all — foie gras, truffle and a rich sauce. It was supposedly invented by Escoffier, who was the first chef at the Savoy and on whose original coal-fired stoves I was still working.

The classic sauce is made with a demi-glace, a much-reduced stock and flour-based sauce. In this method the sauce is lighter, but a good rich stock is essential (see page 252).

SERVES 4

4 slices of good white
  bread
85 g/3 oz/6 tbsp cold
  butter, cubed
4 fillet steaks
salt and pepper
4 small slices of foie gras
  (about 85g/3 oz each),
  no more than 1cm/^{1}/$_2$ in
  thick
2 shallots, finely chopped
2 tbsp red wine
200 ml/7 fl oz/generous
  ^{3}/$_4$ cup reduced stock
  (see page 252)
4 tbsp dry (Sercial or
  Verdelho) Madeira
4 slices of fresh truffle

To make the croûtes, cut out discs of bread the same diameter as the steaks. Heat 55 g/2 oz butter until foaming and fry the croûtes until golden brown on both sides. Drain on kitchen paper and set aside.

Prepare the steaks (see pages 42–43) and cook in a very hot frying pan. Remove from the pan and leave them in a warm place to rest. Cook the foie gras in the same pan for about 5 seconds on each side – just to colour. Remove and place on top of the steaks to keep warm.

Reduce the heat and sweat the shallots in the same pan until softened and slightly coloured. Add the red wine and reduce to a glaze, then add the stock and Madeira and simmer until reduced by half. Swirl in the remaining cold butter, taste for seasoning and strain through a fine sieve.

Place the foie gras-topped steaks on the croûtes of bread, top with a slice of truffle, pour over the sauce and serve immediately.

Tips

• Foie gras can be hard to come by: you could use calves' liver, duck liver or free-range chicken liver instead. Alternatively, use canned pâté de foie gras.

• Don't skimp on the butter when making the croûtes: if they are not crisp, they will soak up all the sauce!

Carpetbag steak

Australians claim this dish as their own, but oysters and beef have been combined for centuries – steak and oyster pie (see page 138) is traditional in both Scotland and England. Carpetbag steak was described in an Indiana newspaper in 1891, suggesting that the recipe was already well known in the United States, and I believe the name comes from a pejorative term for Americans from the north who travelled to the south after the American Civil War, ready to make a quick buck: they often carried large bags made from carpets. The steak stuffed with oysters resembles just such a bag! Ideally, ask your butcher for a seam-cut rump, which is meat from a single piece of muscle.

SERVES 4

4 rump steaks,
  3–4 cm/about 1¹/₂ in
  thick
8 oysters
salt and pepper
1 tbsp olive oil
55 g/2 oz/4 tbsp butter
2 shallots, finely chopped
2 tbsp dry white wine

Using a sharp knife, cut a horizontal slit in the steaks to form a pocket. Just before you are ready to cook and serve the dish, shuck the oysters, reserving the liquid. Stuff two oysters into each steak and tie or sew up with kitchen string to seal the incision. Pat the steaks dry and season with salt and pepper.

Heat a heavy frying pan (skillet) and when very hot add the oil and a small piece of the butter, then add the steaks and cook to your liking. They need a little more resting time than usual – 6 or 7 minutes – to allow the warmth to permeate to the centre of the meat.

While the steaks are resting, return the pan to a medium heat, add the remaining butter and stir in the shallots. Soften for a few minutes, then add the wine and stir well. Pour in any juices from the rested steaks together with the reserved oyster liquid and heat through, then pour over the steaks and serve at once.

Accompaniments

Best chips

The head chef at the Savoy in my day, Silvino Trompetto, always maintained that the best chips (or *frites*) came from France. I am sure this was to do with potato variety, and the French varieties gave a crisp exterior and fluffy interior. I suggest Maris Piper, as these seem to have just enough dry matter to be fluffy but not so much that they fall apart. However, my colleague Alan Romans, who is an expert on potatoes, says they have different characteristics depending on where they are grown, so it's wise to consider local variations – ask your greengrocer for advice.

SERVES 4
4 large potatoes (about 800 g–1 kg/1¾–2¼ lb), peeled
plenty of beef dripping or oil for deep-frying
salt

Cut the potatoes into 1–2 cm/½–¾ in thick sticks – they should all be the same thickness. Place in a pan of cold water and bring to the boil. Simmer for a few minutes – they should be not quite cooked. Drain carefully so as not to break them and allow to dry thoroughly. This can be done well in advance.

To finish cooking, use either a deep-fat fryer or a large pan less than half full of oil – it will bubble up. Bring the fat to 180°C/350°F, or until a cube of bread browns in 30 seconds. Plunge the chips in and cook for about 2 minutes, until they are golden brown. Depending on the size of the pan, you may need to do this in batches – don't put too many in at once, or else you will end up with a soggy mess! Drain on kitchen paper, sprinkle with salt and serve hot.

Tips

- Many people claim the best cooking medium is beef dripping, and you can find this in butchers' shops and supermarkets. The next best is probably groundnut (peanut) oil.

- Some people prefer not to blanch the potatoes in water first. Instead they initially cook the chips in oil at 160°C/320°F, then drain and finish the cooking at the higher temperature. In my experience, blanching in water removes traces of starch, which is essential to get the chips really crisp.

Onion rings

I love onion rings with a steak or as a snack. I prefer them without a batter, as I think both the crunch and flavour are lost. Here is a simple idea using dried breadcrumbs, which give a really good crunch and the delicious taste of onion.

SERVES 2

groundnut (peanut) oil for deep-frying
1 onion, sliced thinly but kept whole – better to slice thicker than to break the rings!
plain flour seasoned with salt and pepper
1 egg, well beaten
dried breadcrumbs (see Tips)

Fill a deep-fat fryer or a large pan about one-third full of oil and heat to 190°C/375°F, or until a cube of bread browns in 20 seconds.

Dip the onion rings in the seasoned flour, then shake off excess flour. Dip in the egg to coat all over, then dip in the breadcrumbs, making sure the onion is fully coated. Plunge into the hot fat and cook until crisp and brown. Drain on kitchen paper and EAT.

Tips

- To make dried breadcrumbs, blitz leftover bread and crusts in a food processor, then spread them on a baking sheet and allow to dry in a cool oven, 140°C/275°F/gas 1, for about 1 hour. Tip them back into the processor and blitz to a fine texture.

- When beating the egg, use a bowl rather than a small cup, as you need to break up the albumen to get a smooth coating consistency.

- Make sure the egg coats the onion thoroughly, otherwise the breadcrumbs won't adhere fully: you want a complete casing of crust so that the fat doesn't get to the onion itself.

Béarnaise sauce

My favourite sauce to go with a good steak or a chateaubriand (see page 96) or Beef Wellington (see pages 59–60) – the richness of butter and egg yolks is cut through with vinegar and tarragon.

SERVES 4–6

225 g/8 oz/1 cup unsalted butter
several sprigs of tarragon
1 tsp finely chopped shallot
125 ml/4 fl oz/½ cup white wine vinegar
2 tsp chopped fresh parsley
1 tsp chopped chervil (optional)
3–4 egg yolks
salt and pepper
juice of ½ lemon

Melt the butter in a Pyrex jug and set aside so it cools but remains melted and separated into clarified butter and whey.

Remove the leaves from the tarragon stalks and set aside. Roughly chop the stalks and place in a small stainless steel pan with the shallot and vinegar. Place the pan over a low heat and reduce to about 1 tablespoon. Remove from the heat and allow to cool slightly.

Chop the tarragon leaves – you should have about 1–2 tablespoons –and add to the parsley and chervil, if using. Set aside.

Add the egg yolks to the reduced vinegar and shallots and whisk over a low heat until the mixture begins to thicken slightly. The secret is to keep the heat low and take the pan off and on the heat as you whisk so that it heats gently:

too hot, and it will scramble; too cold, and it just won't cook! When the sauce forms a light foam (if you lift the whisk, it will leave a faint trail in the sauce), put the pan on a folded damp cloth. Keep whisking all the time and slowly pour the melted butter into the mixture – start by adding just a few drops at a time. The sauce will thicken as you whisk in the clarified butter. You can leave the white residue behind; or if you feel it's wasteful, then add it as well, to make a more pourable sauce.

It is traditional to strain the sauce through a sieve, making it very smooth, or you could just pick out the tarragon stalks, leaving the chopped shallot. Now add the chopped herbs, check for seasoning and add the lemon juice. Pour the sauce into a jug or bowl and keep warm in a pan or bowl of warm water.

This sauce can be kept warm for up to 4 hours, but make sure the water doesn't get too hot.

Reduction sauces

The most straightforward way to create a delicious sauce in seconds. While the steak is resting, just splash a little wine into the pan to add an extra dimension. First try the red wine (marchand de vin) version, then use your imagination and try port, whisky or cognac – or just stock, perhaps with a little double cream or crème fraîche.

Marchand de vin sauce

In the classic culinary repertoire, marchand de vin is a compound butter made with red wine and other ingredients. However, I like to think of the wine merchant (*marchand de vin*) in the days when wine was sold directly from the barrel. At the end of his busy day he would take a little wine from a cask and use it to finish off his supper.

Once your steak has cooked, remove it from the pan and reduce the heat. Add a splash of red wine and a little beef stock and boil to reduce by half. Swirl in 25 g/1 oz/2 tbsp cold unsalted butter, season to taste and there you have it – a simple sauce to coat your steak.

Flavoured butters

A slice of flavoured butter melting over a hot steak or veal chop is a simple standby 'sauce'. Also excellent with grilled fish or steamed vegetables.

To serve, allow about 15 g/½ oz/1 tbsp per person, but it's easier to make a larger amount: store, well-wrapped, in the fridge or freezer.

Beat 115 g/4 oz/½ cup unsalted butter until softened, then beat in your choice of flavouring (see below). Roll up to form a 3 cm/1¼ in diameter log, wrap in greaseproof (wax) paper and chill for at least 2 hours.

Maître d'hôtel

A classic garnish: beat in 1 heaped tbsp finely chopped fresh parsley, a little grated lemon zest and 2 tsp lemon juice. Season with salt and pepper.

Garlic

Blanch 5 or 6 garlic cloves in boiling water for 5 minutes. Run under cold water, then peel and mash into the butter, together with 1 tbsp finely chopped fresh parsley, salt and pepper.

Anchovy

Surprisingly good with steak or veal: beat in 3 or 4 anchovy fillets (don't overdo it) and season with pepper.

Mustard

Beat in about 3 tsp Dijon mustard.

Tomato and paprika

Ideal with veal: beat in 1–2 tsp paprika (or smoked paprika) and 1 tbsp tomato purée, and season with pepper.

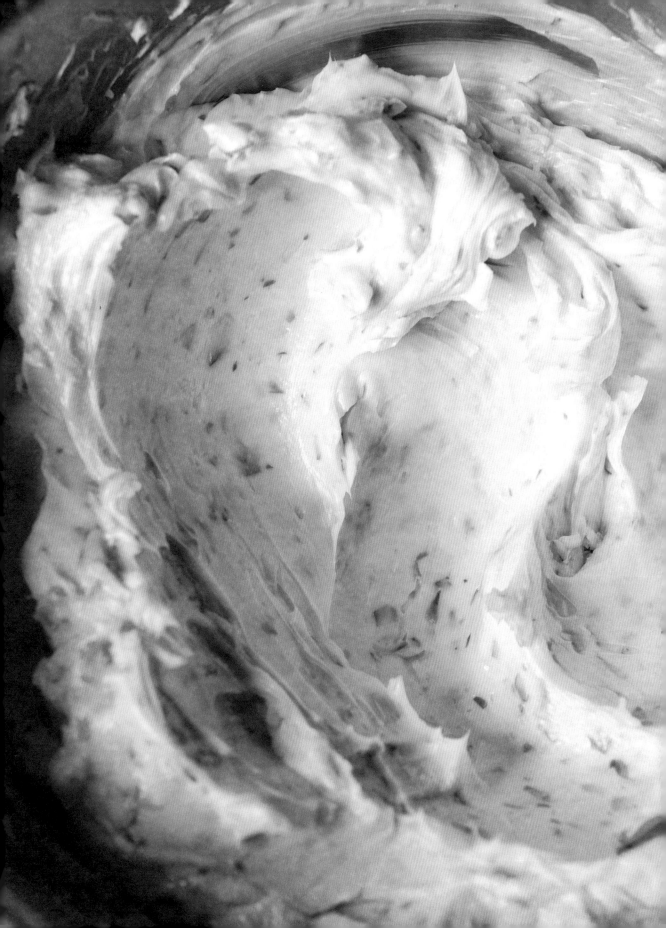

Club sandwich

Entering this realm is fraught with danger, as in the food world people often have a very fixed idea of what they believe is the real deal! Here, I just wanted to flag up the potential of small steak cuts for a luxurious lunch.

SERVES 2

about 200 g/7 oz sirloin or
    ribeye steak
6 pieces of bread (of your
    choice)
mayonnaise
4 gherkins
wholegrain mustard
rocket (arugula) leaves

Cook the steak in a very hot pan (see page 43) and leave to rest for a few minutes while you prepare the sandwich.

Toast the bread lightly on both sides. Spread a little mayonnaise on two slices of toast and slice two gherkins on each one. Spread a little mustard on another two slices and sprinkle a little rocket on each one.

Slice the steak thinly and arrange over the four slices and then sandwich together, with the mayonnaise/gherkin on the bottom. Complete the sandwich with the last piece of toast, press down firmly and cut each one into four diagonally. Hold together with cocktail sticks.

Variations

Steak and blue cheese

Instead of a layered sandwich, slice a baguette three-quarters of the way through, so it opens up like a book. Arrange a layer of sliced Stilton or Dolcelatte cheese on the bottom, cover with small spinach leaves, then top with the sliced steak. Press down firmly and cut into manageable lengths.

Rose veal

Instead of the steak, use 8 thin escalopes of rose veal and cook over high heat for a minute on each side. Rest and create the club sandwich as above. Another delicious variation is sliced rose veal, Parmesan and rocket.

Steak and onion

Thinly slice 1 or 2 onions and cook in a little oil and butter over a low-medium heat for 10-15 minutes, until softened and browned. Serve in a baguette, with sliced steak.

Beef Wellington

The classic fillet of beef wrapped in puff pastry. The secret is to make sure that the beef doesn't exude too much liquid, which would make the pastry soggy: the meat needs to be browned all over and left until cold before you wrap it in pastry. There are many variations, so it's something you can really make your own. Some recipes wrap the beef in pancakes or in prosciutto, although this strikes me as wasteful – it's an expensive bit of blotting paper! Others add a thin layer of pâté between the beef and the pastry. I prefer to make a really dry mushroom mixture, which enhances the rich flavours of this dish.

SERVES 4–6

700 g–1 kg/1 lb 9oz–2¼ lb
  piece of beef fillet
55 g/2 oz/4 tbsp butter
1 large onion, finely
  chopped
125 g/4½ oz firm button
  mushrooms, finely
  chopped
200 g/7 oz fresh spinach,
  finely chopped
salt and pepper
1 egg yolk
400 g/14 oz puff pastry
Béarnaise sauce, to serve
  (see page 55)

Dry the fillet thoroughly with kitchen paper. Melt half the butter in a hot pan and brown the meat all over; you want the meat to be well coloured, which will take about 10 minutes. Set aside and leave until cold.

In the same pan, soften the onion in the meat juices, adding the remaining butter. When soft and golden add the mushrooms and spinach and cook over a low heat, stirring gently, until really dry. This will take 25–30 minutes and you will need to reduce the heat the drier it becomes, otherwise the mixture may catch and burn. When the mixture has reduced to a sort of paste, season well and set aside to cool.

Make an egg wash by whisking the egg yolk with a little water. Roll out the pastry to a rectangle about 35 x 40 cm/14 x 16 in – it needs to be large enough to wrap the fillet with a small overlap. Spread half the mushroom mixture in a line across the centre of the pastry. Then place the fillet flat side up on the mixture. Spread the remaining mushroom mixture over the top of the meat. Using a pastry brush, brush some egg wash along one edge of the pastry. Lift the top and bottom pieces of pastry over the beef: the egg-washed edge should overlap by about 2 cm/¾ in and no more;

Recipe continues
overleaf

Tips

- Ask your butcher for a piece cut from the middle of the fillet so that it is an even thickness all the way along.

- Wash and dry your spinach well in advance.

- Brushing with egg wash several times helps to give a crisp texture and golden-brown glow to the cooked pastry.

- If you like, place the pastry-wrapped fillet on some baking parchment before chilling. When you are ready to cook, place a baking sheet in the oven to get really hot. Then gently slide the Wellington off the parchment directly on to the baking sheet: this allows the pastry on the bottom to start cooking straight away and helps avoid a soggy bottom!

press firmly to seal. Trim the end pieces of pastry, brush with egg wash and seal to enclose the fillet completely.

Carefully turn the whole thing over so the join is underneath and place on a metal baking sheet. Brush all over with egg wash. You can, if you like, decorate the top with pastry trimmings cut into thin strips or other shapes. Egg wash again and chill for at least 30 minutes, but no more than 24 hours.

Preheat the oven to 200°C/400°F/gas 6. When hot, brush the pastry once more with egg wash and bake for 20–25 minutes until golden and crisp. Reduce the heat to 150°C/300°F/gas 2 and cook for another 10 minutes. Remove from the oven and leave to rest for 10 minutes. Slice and serve with Béarnaise sauce.

Beef Stroganoff

This dish has an air of romance and nostalgia, as it reminds me of the great classical kitchens in which I trained. Waiters in coat tails, and lots of cream in the sauces. There's some dispute about the origin of the dish, but to me the name and the use of sour cream are clearly Russian. The fillet steak completes the grand imperial picture. It's a quick dish but should always be done to impress. If fillet steak is too pricey, try rump.

SERVES 4

500 g/1 lb 2 oz fillet steak, cut into strips about 5 cm/2 in long and 1 cm/½ in thick
50 g/1¾ oz/4 tbsp butter
350 g/12 oz button mushrooms, sliced
1 shallot, finely chopped
1 garlic clove, crushed
4 tbsp double (heavy) cream, sour cream or crème fraîche
salt and pepper
1 tbsp chopped fresh parsley

Dry the meat thoroughly on kitchen paper. Heat a large frying pan (skillet) and when very hot add the butter; as it bubbles up, quickly add the meat, scattering it all over the pan so it cooks rapidly. Brown on one side and then turn it, keeping the pan over a high heat. As soon as the meat is browned all over but still very rare, remove from the pan and keep warm.

Add the mushrooms and more butter if required, toss them in the meaty juices until just softening, then add the shallot and garlic and stir to mix. Add the cream and allow to bubble up, add a little salt and pepper to taste, then return the meat to heat through for about 30 seconds. Serve at once, with pilaf rice, sprinkled with chopped parsley.

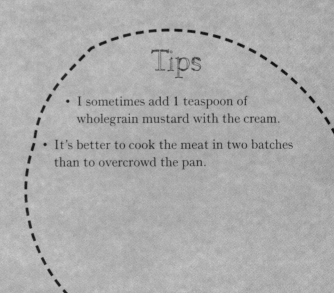

Tips

- I sometimes add 1 teaspoon of wholegrain mustard with the cream.
- It's better to cook the meat in two batches than to overcrowd the pan.

Tip

I know they are expensive, but an electric slicer is brilliant for slicing semi-frozen meat. Above all, don't get a butcher to do this for you, as the meat needs to be eaten within minutes of being sliced.

Carpaccio

Carpaccio was created in Harry's Bar in Venice in 1950 and named after a 15th-century Venetian painter — apparently the brilliant red colours reminded the chef of Carpaccio's paintings. In the original version the thin slices of raw lean beef were drizzled with a creamy mustard mayonnaise. Nowadays 'carpaccio' is used not just for thinly sliced raw beef, but also for venison or tuna, or other fish, and instead of the creamy dressing the dish may be topped with oil and lemon, with shaved truffles or Parmesan. Fillet is the traditional choice of beef, but you may prefer the flavour of sirloin or even a single-seam piece of rump.

High quality is paramount: the best beef, extra virgin oil providing a pungent depth, nutty Parmesan and absolutely fresh rocket or watercress — no limp leaves!

SERVES 4

about 450 g/1 lb top-
  quality lean beef
handful of watercress
  or rocket
50 g/1¾ oz Parmesan
  cheese
100 ml/3½ fl oz/6–7 tbsp
  olive oil
juice of 1 lemon
salt and pepper

Method 1

Slice the meat as thinly as you can and then place each slice between two sheets of clingfilm (plastic wrap) and beat out until the meat is so thin you can almost see through it (I use a rolling pin). Spread the meat over 4 medium-sized (about 20 cm/8 in diameter) cold plates.

Scatter the leaves over the meat and shave some Parmesan finely over the top.

Whisk the olive oil, lemon juice, salt and pepper together to form an emulsion and sprinkle over the leaves.

Method 2

Put your piece of beef into the freezer until it is firm but not solid. You can then cut wafer-thin shavings from it. Mound them on 4 plates and sprinkle with shaved Parmesan. Place the leaves around the outside of the plate and sprinkle with the dressing.

Steak tartare

On no account consider using anything other than the best quality beef you can get for this. It was a classic of the grand kitchens and flamboyant waiters would mix and blend in style at the table; it was as much theatre as food. Nowadays, it's a topic some people get very pedantic about, insisting on this sauce or that ingredient. Of course it is down to personal choice, but if serving as a party dish I think the host should prepare it to their own taste, the only thing left to the guest being the mixing of the egg yolk. The beef itself must be lean and it is essential that it is chopped by hand and not minced, and certainly never prepared in a food processor.

SERVES 4

800 g/1¾ lb top-quality lean fillet, sirloin, topside (top round) or rump
200 g/7 oz shallots, finely chopped
100 g/3½ oz capers, chopped
2 tbsp Worcestershire sauce
a few shakes of Tabasco
2 tbsp chopped fresh parsley
salt and pepper
4 free-range or organic egg yolks
toast, to serve – sourdough bread is good

OPTIONAL INGREDIENTS TO CONSIDER

2 tbsp finely chopped red onion (instead of the shallots)
2 tbsp chopped gherkins
1–2 tbsp olive oil
few drops of brandy
chopped anchovies
touch of grated horseradish

Using a heavy, very sharp knife, finely chop the beef. Mix in the shallots, capers, Worcestershire and Tabasco sauces and the parsley – plus any of the optional ingredients you fancy. Season to taste and shape into 4 mounds, or use a pastry cutter to shape on each plate. Make a small indention in the top and add an egg yolk. Serve with toast.

Tips

- It's worth investing in one of those big flat-bladed Japanese knives, which chop beautifully.

- Try sprinkling Maldon salt or other good coarse sea salt over the finished plate of tartare: the extra crunch is wonderful with the smoothness of the other textures.

Beef fondue

Most of us have heard of Swiss cheese fondue but when I worked in Switzerland I came across a wonderful fondue using beef or veal, sometimes called 'fondue Chinoise'. Instead of melted cheese, the fondue pot is filled with simmering meat stock, into which you dip your skewer of meat, so you can cook it to your liking, then eat with your choice of accompaniments.

SERVES 4–6

800 g/1¾ lb lean beef or
  veal, thinly sliced
2 litres/3½ pints/2 quarts
  good, well-flavoured beef
  or veal stock
small piece of fresh ginger,
  crushed
75 ml/5 tbsp dry sherry

DIPS
soy sauce
sesame oil
mayonnaise mixed with a
  little grated horseradish
mayonnaise mixed with a
  little mustard and lemon
  juice
raw egg yolk
sour cream

ACCOMPANIMENTS
carrots, fennel, courgettes,
  cut into sticks
green salad: watercress,
  rocket, little gem lettuce

FOR THE BROTH
4 tbsp long-grain rice
2–3 heads of pak choi
  (bok choy), shredded

Cut the meat into small slices and place on a serving plate. Put all your dips into small bowls and arrange the vegetables on another plate.

Put about 1 litre/1¾ pints/4 cups of the stock into your fondue pot, together with the ginger and sherry. Put it in the middle of the table and light the burner. Keep it just below a simmer and top it up with more stock if need be. Using a fondue fork, each guest rolls up a piece of meat and dips it in the hot stock to lightly poach. You can either use your skewer to dip the meat into your chosen sauce or transfer the meat to your plate with some crunchy vegetables and a few spoonfuls of dip – but don't eat directly from the fondue fork.

When all the meat is finished, add the rice and shredded pak choi to the broth and simmer for about 15–20 minutes, stirring occasionally, until the rice is cooked. Serve in bowls. While the broth is cooking, serve a crisp green salad.

📷 See picture overleaf.

COOKING OVER FIRE

This brings out the hunter in us – especially men. The summer barbecue may be the only time some of us do the cooking! But the flavours created by bathing food in flames cannot be beaten, and the idea of cooking outside is very appealing; fresh air increases appetite. However, a barbecue can be an unknown quantity, especially when the weather is so unpredictable! While cooking over fire can't be replicated in the kitchen, the searing heat can, and a smoking-hot griddle pan is usually more controllable than a barbecue. Remember to open the windows or put the extractor fan on full.

Burgers are fabulous cooked on the barbie, and so are kebabs: cubes of meat threaded onto a skewer of some kind, whether a flat metal skewer, a bamboo stick or a rosemary stalk – with the latter you have to be careful that it doesn't disintegrate during cooking, but the rosemary does add a great flavour to the meat. Kebabs are a feature of outdoor cooking the world over, from the Greek souvlaki to South-East Asian satay. Sometimes vegetables are interspersed with the cubes of meat.

If using a really tender cut of meat such as fillet, a marinade isn't necessary, but with lesser cuts such as rump or topside (top round) a marinade will help to tenderize the meat. The secret is to get the heat at the correct, high temperature and to turn the skewers regularly to ensure even cooking.

Ginger & garlic kebabs

Here is a delicious Indian-inspired kebab. Serve with salad or cherry tomatoes, or a tomato salsa or spicy salsa verde (see page 253) in naan bread.

SERVES 4

600 g/1 lb 5 oz lean beef
  such as sirloin or rump,
  cut into 2 cm/³/₄ in cubes
vegetable oil

MARINADE
4 tbsp plain yogurt
juice of 1 lemon
25 g/1 oz fresh ginger,
  peeled and grated
1 garlic clove, puréed
¹/₄ tsp ground coriander
4 pinches of salt

Place the meat in a bowl. Combine the marinade ingredients, pour onto the beef and mix thoroughly. Marinate for 8 hours or overnight in the fridge.

An hour before you want to cook the meat, get it out of the fridge and let it come up to room temperature.

Thread the meat onto skewers and brush with oil, then cook on a hot grill for about 3 minutes on each side.

The best burgers

I have always had a love–hate relationship with burgers. I dislike fast-food chains and the way that they manipulate consumers. There is also the fact that burgers can simply be disgusting. It was the Hard Rock café in London, back in the 1970s, that first opened my eyes to how good a burger could be: big, juicy and pink in the middle. The Hard Rock was always a good place to take a date you weren't sure about, as the music was so loud you couldn't hear yourself think, let alone talk, and there was always lots to look at, with rock memorabilia lining the walls. I took my son there recently and although it has changed, the atmosphere was still the same.

I am not sure what goes into the Hard Rock's burgers, but I believe that a little fat is essential; it is also important either to mince your own meat or at least to see exactly what is going into it; I like to add a little chopped onion and fresh parsley. The quality of the bun you use is important too: I don't like sesame buns because they can be dry, and prefer a soft white or brown roll. Once the burger is organized it's the bits that go with it that matter; try a little piccalilli, which has elements of sweetness and crunch. Ketchup and mustard spread on top and bottom of the roll and that's all; no soggy tomatoes!

SERVES 4

800 g/1¾ lb good-quality
  minced beef, such as
  topside or rump, with up
  to 25% fat
1 medium onion, finely
  chopped
2 tbsp chopped fresh
  parsley
salt and pepper

TO SERVE
4 buns or rolls
English mustard
tomato ketchup
8 tsp piccalilli, or more
  to taste

Place the mince in a bowl along with the chopped onion and parsley, season and mix thoroughly. Divide into 4 balls and then press down to create flat patties. Leave to firm up in the fridge for an hour or so.

Slice open the buns and toast on the inside for a few moments over the grill or barbecue; keep warm.

Cook the burgers on a very hot barbecue or griddle pan, allowing them to be bathed in fire briefly if possible. Cook for about 2 minutes on each side: you want the outside to be charred and the inside rare to medium-rare.

Spread some mustard on the bottom halves of the buns and ketchup on the top halves. Put a burger on the bottom half of the bun, top with piccalilli and cover with the top half of the bun.

Satay with peanut sauce

A popular snack in Indonesia, and a great barbecue dish.

SERVES 4

600 g/1 lb 5 oz lean beef
  such as sirloin or rump,
  cut into 2 cm/³/4 in cubes

MARINADE
¹/2 tsp garam masala
1 tsp ground cumin
1 tsp salt
2 tsp brown sugar
juice of 1 lemon

PEANUT SAUCE
175 g/6 oz/1¹/4 cups
  unsalted peanuts
2 shallots, chopped
2 garlic cloves
¹/4 tsp chilli powder
  or cayenne pepper
1 tsp salt
1 tbsp groundnut
  (peanut) oil
juice of 1 lemon
2 tsp lime juice
25 g/1 oz/2 tbsp brown
  sugar
1 tbsp cornflour
  (cornstarch), slaked with
  300 ml/10 fl oz/1¹/4 cups
  water

Mix the ingredients for the marinade in a bowl. Add the meat and marinate in the fridge overnight.

To make the sauce: roast the peanuts in a hot dry frying pan (skillet) until they begin to brown. Set aside and remove the skins if you wish (see Tip). Place in a food processor and blitz until coarsely ground. Add the shallots, garlic, chilli and salt and whizz together for a few minutes.

Heat the oil in a pan over a medium heat, add the peanut mixture and after a few minutes add the lemon juice, lime juice and sugar, then the slaked cornflour (cornstarch) and simmer until the sauce thickens. Transfer to a bowl.

Thread the meat onto skewers and cook on a hot grill for about 3 minutes on each side. Serve with the sauce, with salad.

Tips

• You can remove the peanut skins by rolling them on kitchen paper and shaking the light skins off. I never bother – and the skins contain healthy antioxidants!

• Bamboo skewers are authentic for satay. Look for them in Asian shops or in the barbecue section of supermarkets. You'll need to soak them in water for about 30 minutes before you put them on the grill.

• Taste the sauce: you may need to adjust the flavour with soy sauce, fish sauce or more lime juice.

SLOW BEEF

Roasts

The French gastronomic writer Brillat-Savarin (1755–1826) wrote that anyone can learn to cook, but one must be born knowing how to roast. Cookbooks before and since beg to differ and offer a wealth of advice on roasting. Roasting on a spit next to an open fire demands good judgement to ensure that the meat is cooked through and not burnt on the outside, but for more than a hundred years oven-roasting has been the norm. By 1896, Fannie Farmer, America's great culinary authority, was roasting beef in a hot oven; it was seasoned and dredged with flour, and basted with fat every ten minutes. All her recipes were triple-tested and she was confident anyone could follow them.

Lean meat can cook to juicy succulence if it is first larded or barded. Larding is a technique that goes back many centuries: *Le Ménagier de Paris* (1393) mentions larding with bacon. Pieces of pork or beef fat are cut into thin strips and inserted into the meat: in old illustrations you often see roasts that look like a hedgehog, evenly spiked with pieces of fat. With today's tender beef it is rarely necessary, although larding is recommended when roasting venison and very lean beef. Barding means tying a thin piece of fat around the meat: as the fat melts in the heat it bastes the meat.

As well as the cuts shown here, the term 'roast' is sometimes used for certain lean but less tender cuts. Rather than oven-roasting at high temperature they are best pot-roasted. The meat is first browned, some liquid is added and the tightly covered pot is left to simmer for several hours.

1 → **Topside** (**top round**) is a lean, fine-grained boneless cut from the inside of the leg/top of the hindquarters. In the UK it is often sold ready for roasting: rolled with a piece of barding fat tied around it to baste it and keep it moist as it cooks. Suitable for pot-roasting and braising, it can also be sliced thinly and used for beef olives and stir-fries.

2 → The **loin**, or **sirloin**, provides some of the finest roasts. It can be roasted on the bone, or boned and rolled.

3 → The **fore rib**, **wing rib** or **prime rib** is a very tender, flavoursome cut, interleaved with fat that bastes the meat as it cooks. When roasted on the bone it is known as a standing rib roast; for a family dinner, ask your butcher to cut a two- or three-rib piece. The rib can also be boned and rolled as a roast.

Love meat tender

Cooks have devised various ways to ensure the meat they serve is tender, including simmering it in liquid to keep it moist, cooking it in a sealed pot so it 'steams' in its own juices, pounding or chopping it into small pieces, and basting it with fat as it roasts. Local traditions and ingredients seasoned with the cook's imagination have created tasty beef dishes all around the world.

ROASTING

The roast beef of old England is a symbol of national pride, but how did English beef get its reputation? The magnificent feasts of the Middle Ages were held in princely courts throughout Europe: at marriages and coronations, Christmas and Easter, cooks served up roasted geese, swans and peacocks, along with suckling pigs, venison and huge pieces of beef. In 1420 the Duke of Savoy's master cook, Chiquart, described the necessary provisions for an honorable feast, which needed three or four months of planning. The first item on his list was 100 well-fattened cattle. He also needed 130 well-fattened sheep, 120 pigs and, for each day of the feast, 100 piglets, 200 kids and 100 calves – and countless game animals and birds. Another item on his checklist was '120 iron spits which are strong and are thirteen feet in length', along with dozens of smaller spits. Even these large spits would rarely have been used to roast a whole ox: too heavy and awkward to mount on a spit, it would also have taken too long to cook and carve. *Le Ménagier de Paris* (1393) explains how the Paris butchers cut the cow into four principal parts: shoulders, thighs, front and rear parts of the body. Chiquart also explains how the roast beef should be carved into 'fair and large royal pieces' and served 'on a large gold platter without putting on anything else.' So, no fancy sauces with this roast beef.

There were plenty of opportunities for cultural exchange in the Middle Ages. In times of peace the courts and their entourages travelled from country to country; during wars the kings, knights and soldiers may have spent months abroad. Diplomats, merchants and writers travelled extensively, often recording their observations. French cooks came to work in England and vice versa: Robert May, author of *The Accomplisht Cook* (1660), worked in France for five years. So England's reputation for beef was not created solely from national pride.

The Tudor physician Thomas Cogan (c.1545–1607) wrote: 'Beef is of all flesh the most usual among English men…plentiful throughout this land, before all other countries…insomuch that no man of honour…can be said to have good provision for hospitality, unless there be good store of beef in readiness.'

The sirloin, one of the finest roasting joints, is translated from the Old French *surlonge* – *sur* meaning above, *longe*, loin. The churchwarden's accounts for St Margaret's, Westminster, in 1554 record a 'surloyn of beef, 6s 8d'. A baron of beef is a large joint, consisting of two sirloins attached to either side of the backbone. The term, first recorded in Samuel Johnson's *Dictionary* (1755), is a play on the idea that a 'sir' is below a baron in British nobility. A 'chine' of beef also refers to meat attached to the backbone; it was probably a sirloin that diarist Samuel Pepys received as a gift on Christmas Eve 1662, 'a great chine of beef and three dozen of tongues'.

Robert May, in *The Accomplisht Cook*, gives instructions to roast various cuts of beef: 'a good chine of beef will ask six hours roasting' while for a fillet, the tenderest part of the beef, 'roast it leisurely, & baste it with sweet butter'. We don't know the size of May's 'good chine of beef', but by the middle of the next century Hannah Glasse (*The Art of Cookery made Plain and Easy*, 1747) gave more precise instructions: 'To roast a piece of beef about ten pounds will take an hour and a half, at a good fire. Twenty pounds weight will take three hours, if it be a thick piece; if it be a thin piece, two and a half hours will do it.'

The Swedish naturalist Pehr Kalm spent six months in England in 1748. He noted the excellence of the roast beef but also – despite the number of English cookery books published in the seventeenth and eighteenth centuries – the general lack of cooking skill:

'Roast meat is the Englishman's…principal dish. English roasts are particularly remarkable for…fatness and a delicious taste, either because of the excellent pasture…or some way of fattening the cattle…The

English men understand almost better than any other people the art of properly roasting a joint, which also is not to be wondered at; because the art of cooking as practiced by most Englishmen does not extend much beyond roast beef and plum pudding.'

The fame of England's roast beef was well established in Europe, even if sometimes scorned for its plainness, and by the eighteenth century the French had come up with the nickname *'les rosbifs'* for the English. England's ongoing love–hate relationship with the French can be traced back to 1066. They've always been close neighbours, often at war. In England, French stylishness may be admired one year and ridiculed for its affected airs and graces the next. A period of alliance between England and France effectively ended in 1731. Is it just coincidence that in 1731 Henry Fielding, the English novelist and dramatist wrote a ballad, 'The Roast Beef of Old England', for his play *The Grub-Street Opera*? The song also provided the title, in 1748, for William Hogarth's satirical painting *O the Roast Beef of Old England* (*The Gate of Calais*), which clearly mocks the French.

When mighty Roast Beef was the Englishman's food,
It ennobled our brains and enriched our blood.
Our soldiers were brave and our courtiers were good
Oh! the Roast Beef of old England,
And old English Roast Beef!

But since we have learnt from all-vapouring France
To eat their ragouts as well as to dance,
We're fed up with nothing but vain complaisance
Oh! the Roast Beef of Old England,
And old English Roast Beef!

The tune is still played at formal Royal Navy mess dinners; apparently it was played to call passengers to dinner on the doomed liner *Titanic*.

Leftovers

Frenchman Henri Misson, who wrote an account of his travels in England in 1698, related how 'it is a common practice, even among People of good Substance, to have a huge Piece of Roast-Beef on Sundays, of which they stuff till they can swallow no more, and eat the rest cold, without any other Victuals, the other six Days of the Week'.

The English fondness for roast beef resulted in many recipes using leftover meat. A Victorian ditty went: 'Hot on Sunday, Cold on Monday, Hashed on Tuesday, Minced on Wednesday, Curried Thursday, Broth on Friday, Cottage Pie Saturday'.

Hashes were originally made with chopped fresh meat; the French *hacher* means 'to chop'. In Mrs Beeton's mid-nineteenth century recipes for hashed beef, cold roast beef is gently reheated in a sauce or gravy; she noted that it could be served 'in walls of mashed potatoes browned'. Nowadays a hash usually combines meat and cooked potatoes, fried up until the potatoes begin to brown and crisp. Hachis Parmentier is the French version of cottage pie, named after Antoine Parmentier, who made potatoes popular in Paris shortly before the French revolution. Cottage pie began to appear on English tables in the late eighteenth century: after 1790 it is mentioned several times in James Woodforde's *Diary of a Country Parson*.

Stovies – a thrifty Scottish dish of sliced potatoes cooked with onions and the remains of the Sunday roast – may take its name from the Old French *estuve*, meaning something steamed, or cooked its own juices. The English word 'stew' has the same root.

Mrs Beeton's *Book of Household Management* (1861) includes recipes for curried beef, beef rissoles, which sound worth a try – finely minced leftover beef is mixed with breadcrumbs, herbs, lemon zest and egg, made into little balls and fried until brown – and 'bubble and squeak', made from sliced beef and cabbage, fried in butter. The name is said to come from the sound of the dish cooking in the pan. Mrs B also gives a rather skimpy version of *miroton*; at its best *miroton* gives new life to the beef left over from a *pot au feu*, the French counterpart to an English Sunday roast. The sliced beef is reheated in a well-flavoured onion sauce, sprinkled with fine breadcrumbs and baked.

And if your roast beef is cooked rare, as it should be, so that the interior is still deep pink and juicy, the leftovers can be used for a stir-fry.

Accompaniments

The **gravy** of medieval feasts was a spicy sauce made with ginger and cinnamon, thickened with ground almonds or breadcrumbs. Later, 'gravy' described the juices collected beneath the roasting spit; these were made into various sauces by adding herbs, spices, vinegar, orange or lemon juice, egg yolks or breadcrumbs. By the eighteenth century 'gravy for soups and sauces' was based on a broth of neck, leg or other coarse lean beef. To this day, shin beef is sometimes sold as 'gravy beef' in Australia. Today's gravy is made by deglazing the residue left in the roasting pan with good beef stock and boiling to concentrate the flavours. Flour may be used to thicken the gravy.

Yorkshire pudding, the traditional English accompaniment to roast beef, was originally known as 'dripping pudding' because the batter was cooked underneath the roasting spit, with the hot meat juices dripping into the pudding. It became associated with the English county of Yorkshire in the eighteenth century, possibly because it was popular at Yorkshire coaching inns. In *The Good Companions* (1929), Yorkshire-born J B Priestley's character Jess Oakroyd explains that Yorkshire pudding should be light and crisp and eaten 'straight out o't'oven' before the meat and potatoes. This would also take the edge off appetites and so eke out a small joint of meat at the family table.

Mustard takes its name from the Latin *mustus*: in ancient Rome the spicy-hot seeds were ground and mixed with must (unfermented grape juice). The Romans introduced the plant to Britain and in the spice-mad medieval period it was popular because it grew well in northern Europe and did not have to be imported, unlike other costly spices.

Over the centuries and across many countries the seeds of black, brown and white mustard have been combined with different ingredients to produce a huge variety of distinctive condiments. The texture varies from smooth to grainy, the colour from yellow to dark brown, the taste from the modern mild, sweet American style to the complex, flavoursome French Dijon. English mustard is the hottest of them all. Italy has its own long-standing traditions of sweet/sharp mustards: a recipe for Lumbard (Lombardy) mustard appears in the 'Forme of Cury', compiled in about 1390 by the master cooks of Richard II. To make it, the ground mustard seeds are mixed with honey, wine and vinegar. Today's *mostarda di frutta*, or *mostarda di Cremona*, is a relish made from various fruits preserved in a spicy, mustardy syrup; in Lombardy it is often served with boiled meats.

Horseradish was used medicinally by the ancient Egyptians and Greeks; it simulates digestion and is said to ease bronchitis. The active ingredients and pungency of horseradish are destroyed by cooking, so the fresh root is usually peeled and grated just before it's needed. Mixed with cream and often seasoned with salt and sugar, it's served with oily fish such as salmon and eel, particularly smoked fish, as well as with roast beef.

SLOW-COOKED BEEF

For millennia, boiling in a pot suspended over the fire was an easy, economical cooking method for rich and poor alike. For the wealthy, pottages (soup-stews, some thick, some thin) were just one of many courses of a feast, and often included meat or fish. Meanwhile, the poor filled their cauldrons with onions, leeks, cabbages and herbs, occasionally adding a piece of salted, dried or smoked bacon or beef, or the meat of a worn-out old ox, pounding it first to tenderize it. No potatoes – these weren't widespread in Europe until the middle of the eighteenth century – but grains such as barley and oats would have gone into the pot, along with turnips, parsnips, beans and peas. It may not have been as dreary as it sounds, though: the peasant's pottage may also have included game and wild birds, domestic fowl, and fish from river, lake or sea.

While the main difference in their food was one of quantity, the distinction between rich and poor was not always clear-cut: monasteries, merchants, lawyers, doctors and the better-off farmers were usually well fed. Town folk could expect a wider choice of foods than country dwellers. Animals were specially fattened to supply relatively tender meat to butchers in the towns, whereas in rural areas a working ox or milk cow slaughtered at the end of its life would yield tough meat better suited to slow cooking. And from one animal there are only a limited number of choice cuts for grilling and roasting – the rest need to be gently coaxed to tenderness.

It must have been observed that meat became tender when cooked gently and tougher if it was boiled hard. Temperature control cannot have been easy, but in bigger kitchens at least, cooks could adjust the distance of the cooking pots from the fire. Even in a cauldron standing on the fire, gentler cooking could be achieved: tall earthenware jars or 'jugs' filled with meat and vegetables and placed on a board in the bottom of the cauldron were kept away from the direct heat of the flame. Flat-bottomed pots used the lower heat at the edge of the fire, or the glowing embers after the fire died down.

Much has been written about *pot au feu* (pot on the fire), the archetypal French one-pot meal. It provides a clear soup, boiled beef and vegetables, and hopefully some meat leftover for another meal. *Pot au feu* isn't all that ancient: the first printed references appear in the early nineteenth century. By then, middle-class cooks were cooking on iron stoves; the iron retained its heat for several hours – perfect for the long gentle cooking of *pot au feu*.

A one-pot dinner from Brittany goes a step further, and includes a 'pudding' as well as meat and vegetables. *Kig ha farz* (meat and stuffing) is made with beef, pork knuckle (hock) and vegetables; a large dumpling of buckwheat flour, eggs and cream is boiled in a pudding cloth along with the meat and vegetables.

Another variation on the theme of beef cooked in broth is the Vietnamese soup *phở*. The broth is made by simmering marrow bones, short ribs and other cuts such as flank steak and oxtail for four or five hours. The hot broth is poured over rice noodles, thinly sliced sirloin steak, bean sprouts, coriander (cilantro), chillies and other flavourings. Vietnam was controlled by the French for a century: did someone set out to make *pot au feu* and end up with a bowl of *phở*?

Back in Europe, Vienna's great meat dish – after Wiener Schnitzel – is *Tafelspitz*. This is a piece of sirloin or rump, simmered in an aromatic broth, served with sautéed potatoes and horseradish sauce, the latter made either with apples or with whipped cream. It became popular in the days of the Austro-Hungarian empire, when it was said to be the favourite dish of the Emperor Franz Joseph I, but restaurants today still pride themselves on the quality of their *Tafelspitz*.

Northern Italy's *bollito misto* (meaning simply 'boiled mixed') includes not just beef (brisket, chuck or rump), tongue, veal and calf's head but also *cotechino* pork sausage and chicken. The meats are sliced and served with *salsa verde*, *salsa rosso* and *mostarda di frutta*. The European tradition of all-in-one-pot boiled meat and vegetable dishes also includes Spain's *cocido* (with chickpeas) and Portugal's *cozido* (with rice), both of which include pork, sausages, or whatever comes to hand.

Braising, rather than boiling/poaching, is another way to ensure tender beef. Braising and stewing are general terms for cooking at a low temperature in a sealed pot. Braise (it's the same word in French and English; *brasato* in Italian) gets its name from the coals on which such dishes were once cooked. Stew came into English from the Old French *estuve*, which in turn comes from the Greek *tuphos* 'steam'. There are several French versions of *estouffat* or *estouffade*, and Italian *stufato*.

In some towns and villages, pots of meat and vegetables were cooked in the baker's oven. Bakers usually fire up their ovens in the early hours, so they have fresh bread to sell throughout the day. As the oven dies down, the residual heat is ideal for a slow-cooked dish to be ready in time for lunch. Cholent, the Jewish Sabbath dish of beef, barley and beans, was created in order to avoid cooking on the Sabbath: the pot is placed in a very low oven overnight, becoming tender and ready to eat the next day.

A pot roast is a variation on a braise. The meat is browned to create a rich flavour and then cooked for several hours in a large lidded pan or Dutch oven. *Sauerbraten*, or *Sauerbrode*, is a traditional German beef pot roast. A piece of beef such as brisket or round is marinated with wine, vinegar and spices for several days and then braised. The sauce is finished with crumbled gingerbread and/or sour cream.

Boeuf à la mode ('fashionable beef') has been described as a glorified pot roast. A large piece of beef (rump, topside or round) is cooked for several hours with a calf's foot, wine and herbs in a tightly sealed pot, and served with baby onions and carrots. The calf's foot makes the broth rich and gelatinous; beef à la mode may be served cold, set in a shining jelly with a decorative pattern of cooked carrots. A recipe for *boeuf à la mode* appeared in the groundbreaking book *Le Cuisinier François* (1651) by François Pierre de La Varenne. He was the first chef to record the methods of French classical cooking – a major development from the Italian Renaissance traditions introduced to France in the 1530s – at a time when France was a leader of fashionable taste in Europe. Within two years the book had been translated into English; Italian and German editions followed.

While the English gained a reputation for their tender roasts, the French developed an extensive regional tradition of braised dishes. Some French braises are known as *boeuf à la cuillère*, because they are soft enough to eat with a spoon. Burgundy is famous for its splendid wines and hearty yet sophisticated cooking. The region is also known for its magnificent Charolais beef cattle. These elements combine in *boeuf à la bourguignonne* (or beef bourguignon), a classic of French cuisine in which chunks of beef are cooked slowly with red wine and bacon, with a garnish of mushrooms and baby onions. *Carbonnade flamande*, from Flanders in northern France (and Belgium), is braised with beer and onions.

A *daube* is much the same as a braise, and is often associated with Provence. The meat may be cooked in one piece or cut into chunks, and is cooked with wine and fragrant herbs, often including a piece of orange peel. Tougher cuts of beef are transformed to melting tenderness after four or five hours' cooking. *Boeuf à la gardiane* is a speciality of the Camargue region: a variation of the *daube*, it includes garlic and black olives.

Hungarian goulash, or *gulyás*, was originally the one-pot meal of the Magyar herdsmen: *gulyás* means 'cowherd'. The herdsmen used a *bogrács*, a cast-iron cooking pot hung over an open fire, to cook cubed meat and onions with a small amount of liquid. Before the introduction of red peppers from the Americas, the herdsmen rubbed black pepper into the meat. Paprika (ground dried red pepper), the spice that defines goulash today, arrived in Hungary before 1600. It gives a unique flavour to meat when it is cooked over high heat. Paprika-flavoured dishes, enjoyed by rich and poor alike, became inextricably linked with Hungarian national identity in the mid- to late nineteenth century and since then emigrants and visitors have replicated these soups and stews around the world. In Hungary, the basic thick stew is known as *pörkölt*; with the addition of sour cream it becomes *paprikás*; *gulyás leves*, or herdsman's soup, is more liquid and may contain tomatoes, potatoes and fresh peppers.

Chilli con carne, another dish defined by the use of peppers, is the subject of much heated debate. The word chilli comes from the Aztec word for hot peppers of the genus *Capsicum*, which have been eaten in Mexico since prehistoric times. When the Spanish conquistadors arrived in Mexico in the early sixteenth century, they observed that the Aztecs made a sauce of tomatoes and chillies to go with the beans and corn tortillas that formed the staples of their diet. However, chilli 'con carne' (with meat) is defined by the inclusion of meat, introduced in the early days of cattle ranching in the American Southwest. *Chile con carne, or, The Camp and the Field* (1857), is the title of a book by S Compton Smith relating his experiences as a surgeon in the Mexican–American war after Texas had declared independence from Mexico. In the book he recounts an anecdote of some American volunteers interrupting a troop of Mexican soldiers at supper, who fled to the cover of the chaparral:

> '…*what was most interesting to our hungry fellows…were their steaming pots of* chile con carne, *which, in their hurry to "vamos", they had left upon the embers.*'

Despite this early reference, it seems that chilli con carne became widely popular only after the American Civil War. 'Chili parlors' opened in cities across the United States and regional variations developed. Most include cumin and Mexican oregano; some aficionados insist that beans and tomatoes have no place in a true chili. These days chili – sometimes referred to as 'a bowl of red' – is the Texas State Dish. Cooks compete in strictly judged cook-offs; many use their own secret recipes, combining several different types of chilli pepper, whether for subtleties of flavour or sheer mouthnumbing heat.

Argentina is famed for its juicy steaks, and anecdotes tell of gauchos (cowboys) throwing the tougher cuts and offal to their dogs. But of course Argentina has its own repertoire of slow-cooked beef dishes, including *locro* (a soup-stew made with corn, beans and squash), *puchero* (authentic versions include calf's head or tripe, but today may feature brisket, sausages or chicken) and *carbonada criolla* – a hearty stew of beef, winter squash and corn, often including peaches or other fruit – which is sometimes served in the hollowed-out shell of the squash.

Meat, spices, nuts and fruit such as dates, prunes, lemons and apricots combine in Morocco's tagines (beef is used less often than lamb and chicken). These tagines are a link in a long chain that reaches back to the food of medieval Europe. The Arabs had been at the centre of the trade in spices between Asia and the Mediterranean since before Roman times. After the decline of the Roman Empire spices were lost to much of Europe, but the Muslim conquests extended Arab influence around the Mediterranean, bringing a fresh taste for spices and fruits such as pomegranates, apricots and plums. The end of the eleventh century saw the beginning of two hundred years of Crusades, during which the crusaders introduced spices into the cuisine of northern Europe: black pepper, cinnamon, ginger, galingale, saffron, currants and almonds were cooked with meat, poultry and fish. Sugar was used as a spice to balance the acidic flavours of vinegar, verjuice and wine, but then, as now, it was important not to overwhelm savoury dishes with sweet flavours.

Minced (ground) beef makes the most of every bit of meat from the carcass. Chopped into small pieces, pounded or minced, even tough cuts can cook relatively quickly; minced meat traditionally includes a certain amount of fat, which helps to keep it tender as it cooks. In patties and meatballs, breadcrumbs lighten the mixture as well as making it go further, and the choice of flavouring from herbs, spices and seasonings is almost infinite. A recipe for meatballs, called 'pompys', appeared in an English cookbook around 1430: beef, pork or veal is ground and mixed with egg yolks and plenty of spices, then simmered in broth. America's perennially popular meatloaf is thought to have been introduced by German immigrants in the nineteenth century.

Lasagne has a long history; the name refers to the sheets of pasta rather than to today's ubiquitous dish of pasta layered with a tomatoey meat mixture and béchamel sauce and baked in the oven. In ancient Rome, *lagani* were strips of flour-and-water dough, mentioned by Cicero in the first century BC; the *lasanum* was a cooking pot. Pasta sellers, *lasagnari*, were established by the late fourteenth century, but at that time pasta was usually sprinkled with cinnamon, sugar and cheese. In England this dish was called 'loseyns'. In his book *Apicio Moderno* (1790) the well-travelled Italian chef Francesco Leonardi included a recipe for 'gatto di lasagne' made with a ragù of sweetbreads and truffles; he also includes an early recipe for Italian tomato sauce. The Italian meat-based sauce *ragù*, from the French verb *ragoûter*, 'to stimulate the appetite', acquired its name in the late eighteenth century. There are now many versions of *ragù*, some using bits of sausage and pork rinds, while those made in more affluent households use minced beef or veal.

Sausages, usually pork, are sometimes a mixture of pork and beef, or sometimes, as Elisabeth Luard (*European Peasant Cookery*, 1986) explains, 'in the beef-loving countryside of Yorkshire, sausages were made with the parts of the animal that could not be roasted.' Her recipe combines lean minced beef, suet and fresh breadcrumbs in the ratio 4:2:1.

Nowadays, toad in the hole is a simple dish of sausages cooked in batter, but it's a dish that has had many incarnations. Eighteenth- and nineteenth-century recipes used pigeons, lamb chops, or steak and kidney in the batter. Thriftier versions used up leftover roast or stewed beef, or mince patties.

In Scotland, square sausage, looking more like a meatloaf, is often made of beef. Sometimes called Lorne sausage, it is associated with Tommy Lorne, a Glaswegian comedian of the 1920s who made it a butt of his jokes. Sliced and fried, it is the ideal shape for a sausage sandwich. In the Shetland Islands, salted and spiced minced (ground) beef is called *sassermaet* and is used to make patties.

THE PERFECT ROAST

There is nothing complicated about roasting a perfect piece of beef. You just need to consider which piece of meat to buy and/or the result you want. It's a skill mastering the timings involved in bringing a lunch together and it is also important to enjoy the cooking process – a large chunk of a Sunday morning can be spent in the kitchen, should you so wish.

ON OR OFF THE BONE

Roasting meat on the bone helps to keep its shape and juicy succulence; many people insist that the flavour is better too. But some cuts, such as topside (top round) or fillet, don't have a bone attached and they can be just as successful.

SIZE AND SHAPE

Every piece of meat is different, not only in size and shape and which bit of the animal it came from, but also in how long the carcass was aged and how the individual joint has been stored – so the rules on timing for cooking beef can never be exact. A long strip of sirloin, for instance, may weigh the same as a large piece of topside (top round), but the sirloin will take less time to cook because it's not so thick and also because it comes from a less hardworking part of the animal.

THE ROASTING PAN

Cheap, thin roasting pans are a waste of money. Invest in a sturdy pan that you can set over direct heat – which you'll need to do when you brown the meat before roasting, and also when you come to make the gravy. Think about the size of joint you'll be cooking most often: the roasting pan should be just large enough to hold it comfortably. If the roasting pan is too big, the expanse of empty pan is likely to dry out and burn, and your gravy will taste burnt rather than deliciously caramelized.

PREPARATION

Long before you start cooking, make sure the meat is at room temperature – about 14°C/57°F – so that when it's in the oven it's actually cooking rather than just 'taking the chill off'. This means taking a joint out of the fridge for as long as 3 hours before cooking, or if it's a really big joint on the bone, the night before. You can use a thermometer with a fine probe, such as a Thermapen digital thermometer, to check the internal temperature.

It is also very important that the meat is absolutely dry prior to cooking. Using a clean cloth or kitchen paper, wipe off all the surface blood or moisture. If you put a wet piece of meat in a hot pan, the first thing that happens is the water evaporates off, which reduces the heat (that's why we humans sweat – it's our body's way of reducing our temperature) and this means the meat won't form the tasty brown crust we are looking for.

TEMPERATURE

The initial browning of the meat is essential because this creates what is known as the Maillard reaction, which gives us the wonderful caramelized flavours and aroma we expect from roast meat. If your joint is a manageable size, you can brown it all over in a roasting pan on the hob. A large joint or one on the bone should be browned in the oven: set your oven as high as it will go about 20 minutes before you need it. Browning the meat in a very hot oven may take 10–20 minutes, depending on size.

Once browned, the meat finishes cooking in a cooler oven to allow the proteins to slowly break down and become tender. So if you've browned the meat on the hob, set the oven to 150°C/300°F/gas 2. If you've browned the meat in a hot oven, turn it down to 150°C/300°F/gas 2 and just leave the meat to cook.

COOKING TIMES

Of course the cooking time will vary enormously with the type of meat and your personal taste, but here's a rule of thumb: after the initial browning, allow 15 minutes per 450 g/1 lb for rare beef or up to 25 minutes per 450 g/1 lb for well-cooked. You are looking for an internal temperature of 50–55°C/120–130°F for rare meat. Use a meat thermometer or a digital temperature probe to check. If you don't have a thermometer, insert a thin skewer into the thickest part of the meat and leave for a few moments, then touch the skewer to your lip: if it's warm, the meat is cooked rare; if it's cold, return the meat to the oven; if hot, the meat is likely to be overcooked. Remember that the temperature will continue to rise while the meat is resting.

RESTING

After you have cooked your roast, the meat needs to 'relax' – during this time all the juices that have been pushed into the middle of the joint slowly permeate back through the flesh, making it more tender and moist. Resting time depends on the size of the joint. The larger the piece of meat, the longer you will need to rest it before carving. Even a small piece of meat will carry on cooking to some extent as it rests.

Keep the resting meat in a warm place but don't cover it, as this will soften the lovely crisp exterior.

Leftovers

Cold roast beef

Roast beef is equally delicious served cold. Creamy horseradish sauce (see page 99) goes well with cold beef, or try piccalilli, a spicy vegetable pickle, or mostarda, an Italian fruity, mustardy concoction.

Sandwiches

Cold beef is excellent in sandwiches: rare roast beef needs nothing more than good brown bread and a smear of English mustard with a little crisp lettuce such as romaine or Little Gem. Cold meats such as brisket or pot roast beef need a little more spice – try horseradish or sauce gribiche – and a good crusty white bread with rocket (arugula), lollo rosso or red oak leaf lettuce.

Rib roast on the bone

Ask your butcher to French-trim the meat: this means cleaning the meat away from the protruding bones. You can add the trimmings to the gravy.

SERVES 6

2-bone rib of beef, about
2–2.7 kg/4½–6 lb
salt and pepper
1 tbsp beef dripping
4 garlic cloves, lightly
crushed
a sprig of rosemary

Preheat the oven to 150°C/300°F/gas 2. Dry the meat and season all over. Heat a roasting pan, add the dripping and then the meat, fat-side down, and brown all over: this may take some time.

Throw in the garlic and rosemary and put the meat in the oven for about 1–1½ hours. When cooked, it should have an internal temperature of about 50–55°C/120–130°F. Leave to rest, uncovered, in a warm place for 20 minutes before carving.

Roast rump of beef with thyme & mustard crust

This is a simply delicious way to keep the moisture in what can be a lean cut of meat. Make sure there is a good layer of fat on the top of your piece of beef. When on holiday in Italy I have made this with wild fennel instead of thyme, as it was growing outside the villa where we were staying.

SERVES 4–6

1.5 kg/3½ lb piece of
   top rump (top round)
2–3 sprigs of thyme
1 tsp coarse sea salt
1 tsp English mustard
2–3 tbsp olive oil

Preheat the oven to 220°C/425°F/gas 7. Cut criss-crosses into the fat of the beef and dry the meat thoroughly all over. Crush the thyme and discard the stalks. Mix the leaves with the salt, mustard and enough oil to form a paste. Rub the paste into the fat of the meat.

Roast on a trivet in a roasting pan until well browned, about 20 minutes, then reduce the oven temperature to 150°C/300°F/gas 2 and cook for about 45 minutes or until cooked to your liking. Leave to rest, uncovered, in a warm place for 10–15 minutes before carving. Serve with grilled vegetables and horseradish sauce (see page 99).

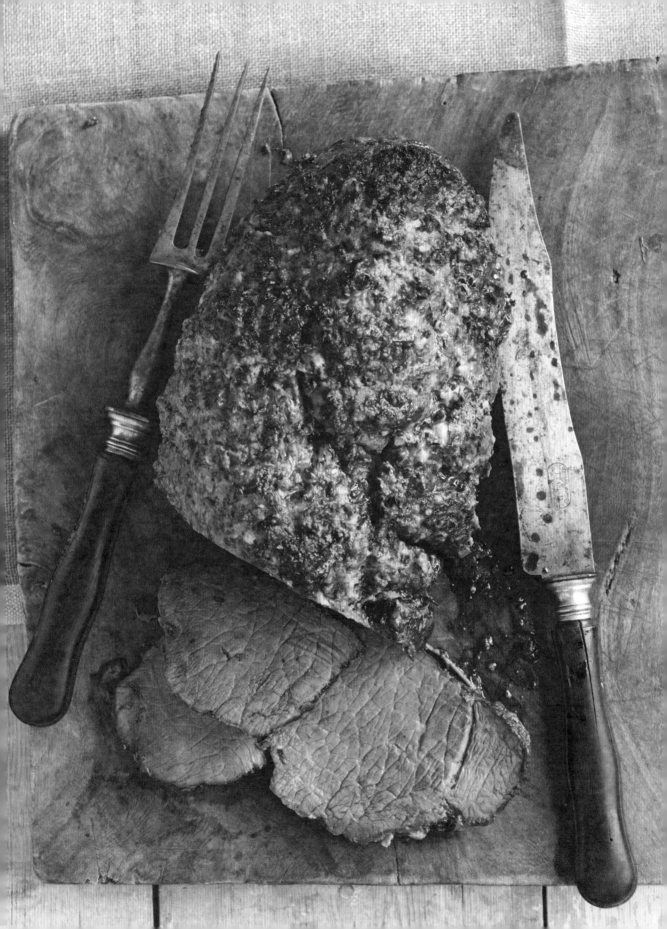

Chateaubriand with tarragon

There is often confusion as to exactly what a chateaubriand is. It is named after an early nineteenth-century French diplomat and writer, and it is a whole piece of fillet, cut from the top end of the fillet. It is usually cooked for 2 people, but it can weigh up to 1 kg/2¼ lb and can serve 4. It should always be served rare.

The sinew needs to be cut away, but leave a little fat and tie the fillet in several places to keep the loose trimmed bits in one piece as it cooks. Your butcher can do this for you. As with any roast, the meat must be at room temperature and completely dry before you season and cook it. Béarnaise sauce (see page 55) is the classic accompaniment to this beef dish, but here is a simpler idea.

SERVES 4

1 chateaubriand, about
   800 g/1¾ lb
salt and pepper
2 tsp olive oil
2 tbsp butter
2 shallots, finely chopped
2 tbsp chopped fresh
   tarragon
100 ml/3½ fl oz/6–7 tbsp
   veal stock
2 tbsp double (heavy)
   cream

Preheat the oven to 180°C/350°F/gas 4. Season the meat with salt and pepper. Heat a heavy-bottomed shallow ovenproof pan over a high heat and add the oil and 1 teaspoon butter; when the butter melts, add the beef. There will be smoke. Turn the meat as each side forms a crust, until it is brown and crusted all over, which will take up to 10 minutes.

Put the pan into the oven for about 10 minutes, depending on the weight of the meat; turn once during the cooking time, then remove from the oven and leave to rest in a warm place for 10–15 minutes.

Meanwhile, pour off the burnt fat, but keep the caramelized juices in the pan, add the remaining butter and soften the shallots over a low heat for about 5 minutes. Add the tarragon and stock and reduce by half, then add the cream and simmer to create a spoonable sauce. Taste for seasoning. Carve the chateaubriand into thick slices and serve with the sauce. Chips are good too!

Accompaniments

Horseradish sauce

Perhaps the most traditional of all sauces on the English table, it has a fiery heat that contrasts with the richness of roast beef. You could 'cheat' by buying a proprietary brand and adding a little double cream. But to do it properly you will need fresh horseradish, which is a difficult root to deal with, as it stains horribly, and it will make your eyes stream! If possible, wear rubber gloves when handling it.

SERVES 4–6

7–10 cm/3–4 in piece of fresh horseradish root
2 tsp lemon juice
1 tsp sugar
1/4 tsp English mustard
225 ml/8 fl oz/1 cup double (heavy) cream, lightly whipped
salt and pepper

Clean, peel and grate the horseradish into a small bowl; you should have about 2 tablespoons. Stir in the lemon juice, which will prevent discoloration. Mix in a little sugar and mustard and fold in the double cream to make a spoonable sauce. Taste for seasoning.

Gravy

A perfect roast deserves a perfect gravy. Make it in the roasting pan while the meat is resting. This will serve up to 6 people; the bigger the joint, the more you need to make – simply increase the amount of flour and stock.

MAKES ABOUT 300 ML/10 FL OZ/1 1/4 CUPS

1 onion, roughly chopped
1 carrot, roughly chopped
1 celery stalk, roughly chopped
1 tbsp plain (all-purpose) flour
a good splash of red wine (2–4 tbsp)
about 600 ml/20 fl oz/2 1/2 cups stock or water
a sprig of thyme
a few parsley stalks
salt and pepper

While the meat is resting, place the roasting pan over a low heat and add the chopped onion, carrots and celery. Stir to colour the vegetables and scrape up the caramelized juices from the roast. Sprinkle in the flour and stir well to mix with the beef juices and vegetables; be brave and let this process go on for a few minutes – you want the flour to really cook out and colour.

Add the red wine and stir well as it bubbles up, then add the stock or water and the herbs. Allow the mixture to simmer gently for about 10 minutes, then strain into a clean pan and simmer to reduce to a pouring consistency. Season to taste.

Yorkshire pudding

My wife is a Yorkshire lass and her parents used to serve the pudding before the beef with a competition between her and her siblings – whichever child could eat the most pudding got the most beef. Of course, by the time they had eaten all the puddings, they didn't want much beef! If you prefer individual Yorkshire puddings they take 15–20 minutes to cook.

In Yorkshire these are not always served with roast beef; they can be eaten with gravy alone – onion gravy (see page 133) is especially good. Alternatively try chopping up sharp cooking apples and stirring them into the batter before cooking – great with sausages.

My recipe includes water because I think this helps to give a crispness to the batter. The important thing is to keep everything hot: hot pan, hot fat and hot oven.

SERVES 6–8

115 g/4 oz/1 cup plain (all-purpose) flour
2 eggs
150 ml/5 fl oz/²/₃ cup full-fat milk
150 ml/5 fl oz/²/₃ cup water
pinch of salt
4 tbsp beef dripping

You can mix the batter by hand: sift the flour into a bowl, break in the eggs and beat with a whisk, then gradually whisk in the liquids and add a pinch of salt. Alternatively, use a blender, in which case put the eggs in first, then the flour and lastly the liquid and salt, whizz to combine and strain through a sieve. Leave to rest for at least 30 minutes before cooking.

Preheat the oven to 220°C/425°F/gas 7 and heat 2 small roasting pans, about 27 x 18 cm/11 x 7 in. When the oven is hot, put about 2 tbsp dripping into each pan and return to the oven for 5 minutes. Carefully tilt the tins to make sure that the fat has coated the sides, then pour in the batter and return to the oven for about 25 minutes, until risen, crisp and browned. Serve at once.

A simple pot roast

This is a great way to cook a less tender cut of beef: the meat juices combine with the vegetables and cooking liquid to keep it moist and flavoursome.

SERVES 4–6

about 1.5 kg/3½ lb piece
 of topside (top round)
 or silverside
salt and pepper
1 tbsp olive oil
2 onions, chopped
2 carrots, chopped
2 leeks, chopped
a sprig of thyme
1 bay leaf
1 head of garlic, cut in
 half horizontally
about 500 ml/18 fl oz/
 2 cups beef or veal stock

Preheat the oven to 150°C/300°F/gas 2. Dry the meat thoroughly and season all over. Heat a casserole dish over a high heat, add the oil and brown the meat all over. Remove the meat and set aside.

Brown the onions, carrots and leeks in the casserole, then sit the beef on top, add the herbs and garlic and pour in enough stock to come about a third of the way up the beef. Bring to a simmer, cover with a tight-fitting lid and cook in the oven for about 2½ hours, basting from time to time.

When cooked, the meat should be very tender. Lift the meat onto a warm plate and leave to rest. Boil the liquid to reduce slightly, then strain through a sieve, pushing the vegetables with the back of a ladle: this will give a slightly thickened gravy. Season to taste. Cut the meat into thick slices and serve with its gravy, along with boiled or mashed potatoes.

Variations

Replace about half the stock with a fruity red wine, beer (ale or dry stout) or dry cider. Don't worry if you haven't much stock: water will do, as the vegetables and herbs give flavour.

Pot roast beef with wild garlic pesto

The beef is coated in a wonderfully pungent wild garlic crust. It really is worth waiting for the wild garlic season for this. Use whatever root vegetables you have to hand, but here I have gone for a variety of colours and shapes.

SERVES 4

800 g/1¾ lb piece of
  topside (top round)
salt and pepper
2 tbsp rapeseed (canola)
  oil
6 small waxy potatoes such
  as Ratte or Belle de
  Fontenay, scrubbed,
  but not peeled
3 parsnips, cut into lengths
12 small shallots, peeled
1 celeriac, peeled and cut
  into chunks

good handful of wild garlic
  leaves, finely chopped
1 tsp smooth mustard
1 tsp paprika
½ tsp sea salt
2–3 sprigs of thyme
350 ml/12 fl oz/1½ cups
  beef stock
200 ml/7 fl oz/generous
  ¾ cup red wine
4 tbsp wild garlic pesto
  (see recipe opposite)
4 tbsp sour cream

Preheat the oven to 150°C/300°F/gas 2. Dry the meat thoroughly and season all over. Heat the oil in a large flameproof casserole dish and brown the vegetables in batches. Once they're browned, set them aside. Add the beef and brown it all over. Remove the beef from the casserole, mix the wild garlic with the mustard, paprika and sea salt and spread all over the beef. Return the vegetables to the casserole and strew with sprigs of thyme. Put the beef on top of the vegetables. Add the stock and wine, bring to the boil, cover with a tight-fitting lid and cook in the oven for about 1½–2 hours.

Wild garlic pesto

55 g/2 oz walnuts
large bunch of wild garlic leaves, roughly torn
55 g/2 oz Cheshire or pecorino cheese, grated
150 ml/5 fl oz/²/₃ cup olive or cold-pressed rapeseed oil
salt and pepper

Heat a small pan and lightly toast the nuts. Leave to
cool slightly. Grind the nuts with the wild garlic and
cheese in a pestle and mortar, gradually adding the oil
until you have a thick, spoonable mixture. Season to
taste – it won't need much salt.

• Wild garlic is usually in season from late
  April to late May. If you can't get it,
  Trotter's Independent Condiments
  (trottersindependent.co.uk) makes
  an excellent wild garlic pesto.

When the meat is tender, scoop out the meat
and vegetables using a slotted spoon, and keep
warm. Bring the cooking liquid to the boil to reduce
slightly. Taste for seasoning, then strain into a warmed
jug. Mix the wild garlic pesto with the sour cream. Place all the
vegetables on a large serving plate. Carve the beef in thick slices and add
to the vegetables. Serve with the gravy and the pesto cream.

See picture overleaf.

Stovies

The great Scottish leftover dish — there is nothing nicer than this dish on a cold evening or after a football or rugby match. Just shove it in the oven to heat through and tuck in. If you have leftover gravy, that tastes great mixed in too!

SERVES 4

1 tbsp beef dripping
2 large onions, sliced
750 g/1 lb 10 oz large floury (starchy) potatoes, such as Maris Piper, Red Duke of York or Desiree, evenly sliced
125 g/4½ oz cold cooked beef, sliced thinly
salt and pepper
300 ml/10 fl oz/1¼ cups beef stock

Preheat the oven to 190°C/375°F/gas 5. Melt the dripping in a frying pan, throw in the onions and cook gently until softened and lightly browned. Take a casserole dish and fill with a layer of sliced potatoes, then the meat, then the onions, seasoning as you go. Pour in the stock. Bake in the oven for about 50 minutes, until the liquid is absorbed and the edges of the potatoes are browned.

Cottage pie

A classic British leftover dish, made from minced cooked beef. I use a fork to create rough peaks in the mashed potato – they crisp up in the oven, ensuring a wonderful crunchy contrast to the smooth mash underneath.

SERVES 4

1 tbsp vegetable oil
1 onion, chopped
450 g/1 lb cooked beef, minced or chopped into small pieces
2 tsp plain (all-purpose) flour
150 ml/5 fl oz/²/₃ cup beef stock
1 tbsp tomato purée
1 tbsp Worcestershire sauce
1 tbsp chopped fresh parsley
salt and pepper
800 g/1³/₄ lb floury (starchy) potatoes, such as Arran Victory, cut into large chunks
40 g/1¹/₂ oz/5 tbsp butter

Heat the oil in a heavy-bottomed pan, sweat the onion gently for about 10 minutes, then increase the heat and add the minced beef. Brown all over, then add the flour and stir in the hot stock. Bring to the boil, then add the tomato purée, Worcestershire sauce, parsley and salt and pepper to taste. Simmer for about 15 minutes. Pour into an ovenproof dish.

Meanwhile, preheat the oven to 180°C/350°F/gas 4. Put the potatoes in a pan and cover with cold water, bring to the boil and simmer for 5 minutes. Drain off all but 1 tbsp water and steam in the oven until the potatoes are tender, then drain well. Mash with the butter, season to taste and spread over the meat. Cook in the oven for 40 minutes until hot through and lightly browned.

CASSEROLES

The casserole is the name of both the food and the receptacle in which it's cooked. The most versatile type is a flameproof cast-iron or heavy-bottomed stainless steel pan with small handles and a well-fitting lid.

A lot has been said and written about the differences between a casserole, stew, braise or pot roast, but what they have in common is that the key to success is to keep the heat very low. The liquid should never boil but should be kept at a gentle simmer, with just the occasional bubble rising to the surface. This slow cooking allows the gelatinous connective tissue between the meat fibres to dissolve, leaving tender meat and a rich sauce. If the temperature gets too high, the proteins in the meat fibres coagulate and become tough before the connective tissue has a chance to dissolve. If your oven is on the hot (or cool) side, you can adjust the temperatures given in these recipes by about 5–10°C/10–20°F.

Professional chefs often use a cartouche to keep the moisture in slow-cooked dishes. It's just a disc of greaseproof (wax) paper that's cut to fit snugly in the pan over the meat — it really helps to keep the meat moist and tender.

Beef bourguignon

This classic French recipe is a must for any beef lover. It can be prepared in advance and reheated, so it's an ideal party dish. The cooking wine should ideally be from Burgundy, and you can sometimes find decent basic red Burgundy at a reasonable price, but you could use any rich but not too tannic wine such as Chianti or an Australian red.

SERVES 6

4 tbsp olive oil

100 g/3½ oz unsmoked bacon lardons

1.5 kg/3½ lb stewing beef, cut into 4 cm/1½ in cubes

3 tbsp seasoned flour

25 button onions or small shallots, peeled (see Tip)

300 g/10 oz button mushrooms, kept whole if small or quartered

1 tbsp tomato purée

300 ml/10 fl oz/1¼ cups red wine

300 ml/10 fl oz/1¼ cups beef stock

thyme, parsley stalks, 2 bay leaves

Heat a large casserole dish and add 1 tbsp olive oil. When hot add the bacon and brown quickly, set aside. Roll the beef in the seasoned flour. Add a little more olive oil to the pan and brown the meat, in batches if necessary – make sure you keep the heat high and don't crowd the pan. Set aside.

In the same pan, quickly brown the onions, followed by the mushrooms, and set them aside together. Stir in the tomato purée and then the red wine and scrape up the juices as the wine bubbles up. Add the stock and herbs, and return the bacon and beef to the pan. Simmer over a very low heat or cook in the oven at 150°C/300°F/gas 2 for about 2 hours or until tender.

When the meat is nearly cooked, add the mushrooms and onions for the last 20 minutes. Using a slotted spoon, scoop out the meat and vegetables and keep warm. Strain the cooking liquid into another pan; it should be a lovely coating consistency, but if it's too thin, boil rapidly for a few minutes. Taste and season. Pour over the meat and vegetables and serve hot.

Tips

- Any stewing meat can be used, but try to avoid too much sinew. Remember that cuts such as chuck or blade will require longer cooking than top rump (top round).

- To peel lots of little onions or shallots, blanch them in a pan of boiling water for 5–10 seconds, then drain and cool under the cold tap. Drain and slip off the skins.

Tagine with prunes & honey

On a recent trip to Morocco I experienced the wonderful method of cooking in a tagine, a shallow earthenware pot with a conical lid, in which all the ingredients are mixed together with minimum liquid and then cooked over a fire.

Out in Essaouira, on Morocco's Atlantic coast, it is much less busy than in the bigger cities and you can enjoy meandering through the streets without the constant tugging at your sleeves of insistent vendors. We looked into a tiny shop that turned out to be a café with a long cooking range covered in tagines, all cooking lunch for different people who would either come to collect them or would have them delivered.

SERVES 4–6

1 kg/2¼ lb stewing beef, diced
2 tbsp olive oil
½ onion, finely chopped
1 tsp ground ginger
2 tsp ground cinnamon
a pinch of saffron threads, soaked in 2 tbsp boiling water
salt and pepper
400 g/14 oz ready-to-eat stoned prunes
2 tbsp runny honey
1 tbsp sesame seeds
4 tbsp roughly chopped fresh coriander (cilantro)

Put the beef, olive oil, onion, ginger, cinnamon, saffron and its soaking liquid in a tagine or casserole dish. Add a good grinding of black pepper, half the prunes, the honey and 6–8 tbsp water. Cover the meat with a disc of greaseproof (wax) paper and place a disc of foil under the lid to seal the pan. Simmer over a very low heat or cook in the oven at 150°C/300°F/gas 2 for 1 hour.

After 1 hour add the remaining prunes, a little salt and the sesame seeds. Reduce the oven temperature to 120°C/250°F/gas ½ and cook for another 1½ hours – or continue simmering for the same time. Taste and adjust the seasoning. Sprinkle with fresh coriander and serve hot with couscous.

Carbonnade flamande

The Belgians and the northern French both claim this as their own. If you want to be authentic, use a Flemish beer, although any beer will do. The addition of a little brown sugar and vinegar really deepens the flavours, and it's quite different from beef cooked in red wine.

SERVES 4

800 g/1¾ lb piece
  of topside (top round)
2 tbsp beef dripping
  or vegetable oil
3 onions, sliced
4 garlic cloves, crushed
salt and pepper
bay leaf
sprig of thyme
200 ml/7 fl oz/generous
  ¾ cup beef stock
500 ml/18 fl oz/2 cups
  Belgian brown ale
2 tsp potato starch or
  cornflour (cornstarch)
1 tbsp red wine vinegar
2 tsp brown sugar

Preheat the oven to 160°C/325°F/gas 3. Cut the beef into slices about 1 cm/½ in thick and 4 x 8 cm/1½ x 3 in. Dry thoroughly. Heat the fat in a large frying pan (skillet) and brown the meat on both sides; do this in batches to keep the pan hot. Remove the meat and set aside. Reduce the heat and add the onions, stirring occasionally until lightly coloured. After about 10 minutes, stir in the garlic, remove from the heat and season with salt and pepper. Lift out the onions, using a slotted spoon.

Place half the meat in a flameproof casserole dish and season lightly. Spread half the onions over the beef, adding the bay leaf and thyme. Cover with the remaining meat and onions and a little more seasoning. Heat the stock in the frying pan and scrape up any residue, pour over the meat and add enough beer to just cover the meat. Bring to the boil, then cover and cook in the oven for 2–2½ hours or until tender.

Drain the cooking liquid into a pan and bring to the boil. Mix the potato starch or cornflour (cornstarch) with the vinegar until smooth and add to the cooking liquid, together with the sugar. Simmer for a few minutes, then pour over the meat and heat through gently. Serve hot, with mashed potatoes or noodles – although in Belgium they'd probably serve frites!

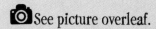 See picture overleaf.

Once you've finished layering the beef and onions, pour on the beer and enjoy the aroma (left picture). After cooking for another couple of hours, you'll be left with this mouthwateringly tasty supper (right picture).

Shin of beef with red wine & rowan jelly

Inspired by a Scottish winter, this casserole uses 'wild things', but not to worry if you can't source them. While rowan jelly is particularly Scottish (the rowan is the fruit of the mountain ash), you can use redcurrant jelly instead. When in season, chanterelles are available from most good delis; you could use ceps (porcini) instead. No thickening agent is required because the meat from the shin provides plenty of luscious richness. This is best made a day or two in advance, so the flavours mellow.

SERVES 4–6

2 tbsp butter
2 onions, chopped
4 celery stalks, chopped
1 kg/2¼ lb sliced beef shin
2 tbsp olive oil
½ bottle of fruity red wine, such as Merlot
2 tbsp red wine vinegar
1 tsp ground ginger
½ tsp freshly grated nutmeg
¼ tsp ground mace
10 juniper berries
2 tbsp rowan jelly
225 g/8 oz fresh chanterelles
salt and pepper

Preheat the oven to 150°C/300°F/gas 2. Heat the butter in a casserole dish over a medium heat and soften the onions and celery. Dry the meat thoroughly. Heat a heavy-bottomed pan, add the olive oil, then brown the meat all over and add to the casserole. Deglaze the pan with a little red wine, then add this wine and all the other ingredients to the casserole. Bring to the boil and season. Cover with a well-fitting lid and put in the oven for 2–2½ hours, until tender. Serve with mashed potatoes.

Tip

Chanterelles and ceps (porcini) are also available dried. For this recipe, you will need about 40 g/1½ oz dried mushrooms. Reconstitute them by pouring on boiling water and leaving until cool. Add a little of the soaking liquid to this casserole and use the rest in a risotto.

Pot au feu

This old-fashioned dish remains popular in French bistros during the winter months. The traditional version is more complex and uses various inexpensive cuts of beef – and sometimes pork and other meats as well – but with a good piece of meat and a variety of vegetables it's a great all-in-one-pot dish.

SERVES 8

2 kg/4½ lb piece of
  beef, such as brisket
  or silverside
1 veal knuckle (shank)
  bone, sawn in half
  widthways
beef or veal stock or water
2 carrots, sliced at an angle
2 leeks, sliced at an angle
1 onion, studded with
  6 cloves
1 head of garlic
1 bouquet garni (2 sprigs
  of thyme, 1 large bay leaf,
  8 black peppercorns and
  several parsley stalks, tied
  together in a piece of
  muslin (cheesecloth))
8 small potatoes
8 shallots, peeled
1 green cabbage, divided
  into 4 wedges but still
  held together near the
  stem
seasonal green vegetables,
  such as mangetout (snow
  peas) or green beans

Place the beef and the knuckle in a very large pot and add stock or water to just cover the meat. Bring to a simmer, then turn the heat right down: you want to keep it at just a gentle simmer. Skim off any froth and add the carrots, leeks, onion, garlic and bouquet garni. Simmer for about 3–3½ hours, topping up the liquid if necessary.

Using a slotted spoon, remove the leeks and carrots, cover and set aside. Judge the time the remaining vegetables will need to cook: add the potatoes to the pot first, then the shallots and lastly the green cabbage, which will need about 10 minutes to cook.

Remove the meat, bone and vegetables from the stock and strain the liquid into a separate pan. Bring to a rolling boil and cook any other green vegetables, such as mangetout or green beans. Remove the marrow from the veal knuckle and stir into the stock to thicken slightly. Cut the beef into good chunks and serve in big bowls with a mix of vegetables and plenty of hot broth poured over. Serve coarse sea salt, cornichons and Dijon mustard separately.

Tip

Instead of a whole veal knuckle (shank), ask your butcher for 8 pieces of marrow bone, sawn into 5–6 cm/about 2 in pieces. Wrap the bones in muslin (cheesecloth) so the marrow doesn't fall out during cooking. Add to the simmering stock for the last hour or so of cooking time.

Boiled beef & dumplings

This classic British dish had to find a place here. This version is from Fergus Henderson's wonderful book *Nose To Tail Eating*, a regular source of inspiration. The original recipe suggests using salted brisket (unrolled and rinsed), but I prefer fresh silverside. I've also added a sprig of rosemary. It relies on root vegetables to give it its earthy rustic flavours. It's a big, generous piece of meat and there will be leftovers.

SERVES 6

2.5 kg/5½ lb silverside
parsley, thyme and
  rosemary, tied together
  with string
2 bay leaves
10 black peppercorns
3 celery stalks, cut in
  half at an angle
6 small onions, peeled
6 carrots, peeled
6 leeks, trimmed

DUMPLINGS
100 g/3½ oz shredded beef
  suet
225 g/8 oz/1¾ cups self-
  raising flour
pinch of salt
1 egg, beaten

Place the beef in a large pot, cover with water, and add the herbs, peppercorns and celery. Bring to the boil and skim, then reduce to a gentle simmer – the water should be barely moving – for about 4 hours.

After about 2 hours add the onions; after 2½ hours add the carrots; and after 3 hours add the leeks. They need to be well cooked, but don't let them overcook – remove them if they are ready before the meat is tender. When all is cooked, remove the meat and vegetables to a serving plate with a little of the broth and keep warm.

To make the dumplings, mix the ingredients together, adding some cold water to create a sticky dough. Shape into walnut-sized pieces, bring the broth to a rolling boil, then drop the dumplings in and cook for about 10 minutes.

Cut the beef into generous slices and serve with the vegetables, dumplings, a little of the broth and horseradish sauce (see page 99).

Dumpling variations

Give your stews a little lift by varying the flavours in the dumplings, but avoid overkill – in other words, don't offer horseradish as a side dish if you have put it in the dumplings!

Herbs

Add a few chopped fresh herbs or dried herbes de Provence to the basic mix.

Lemon

Some grated lemon zest will add a real freshness to the dumplings.

Mustard

Add 1 tsp mustard powder and use 1 tsp wholegrain mustard mixed with slightly less water than you would in the basic recipe.

Horseradish

Add 1 tbsp grated horseradish to the basic mix.

Cheese

Add 1 tbsp grated Cheddar or other hard cheese to the mixture – this goes well with beef and vegetable stews.

Paprika goulash

When I worked in Switzerland, 'Madame', the hotel owner, who disliked green peppers, said they were fit only for cattle. On reflection, I think she was right. I bring this up because the recipe I originally used for this dish calls for green peppers: I have replaced them with red ones, and the colour and flavour are so much better!

SERVES 4

700 g/1 lb 9 oz stewing steak, such as chuck or blade, cubed

2 tbsp seasoned flour

2 tbsp oil, lard or dripping

2 red peppers, deseeded and sliced

2 onions, chopped

1½ tbsp paprika

1 garlic clove, crushed

1½ tbsp tomato purée

300 ml/10 fl oz/1¼ cups stock

bay leaf

sprig of thyme

2 large ripe tomatoes, blanched, peeled and sliced

salt and pepper

Preheat the oven to 160°C/325°F/gas 3. Toss the meat in the seasoned flour. Heat the oil in a heavy ovenproof pan and cook the meat over a high heat, in two or three batches, until golden brown all over. Remove the meat from the pan and set aside.

In the same pan, cook the peppers for a few minutes until softened, then set aside. Reduce the heat and cook the onions until softened. Stir in the paprika and garlic and cook for 1 minute. Add the tomato purée and the stock and stir thoroughly, return the meat to the pan and add the bay leaf and thyme, bring to the boil and cover with a well-fitting lid. Cook in the oven for 1½ hours or until the meat is tender.

Add the reserved peppers and the tomatoes and cook for a further 15 minutes. Serve with mashed potatoes or noodles.

Chile con carne

I have heard an alarming reference to an early version of this dish: the Aztecs in Mexico, confident of victory over a band of Spanish conquistadors, had huge pans of tomato sauce and chilli peppers ready to celebrate victory. The only thing they needed was meat – to be supplied by the defeated Spanish, literally in person!

I prefer to use meat from a fairly lean stewing cut; cubed meat is so much better than minced (ground) and adds a great bite. You can stir in a couple of chunks of dark chocolate at the end to give it extra richness.

SERVES 4

2 tbsp olive oil
700 g/1 lb 9 oz lean
  stewing beef, such as
  blade or shin, cut into
  1 cm/¹/₂ in cubes
1 large onion, chopped
1 fresh red chilli, deseeded
  and chopped
2 garlic cloves, crushed
1 red pepper, deseeded
  and chopped
1–2 tsp chilli powder
1 tsp paprika
1 tsp ground cumin
200 g/7 oz canned chopped
  tomatoes

1 tbsp tomato purée
225 g/8 oz cooked red
  kidney beans, or a
  drained 400 g/14 oz can
salt
2 squares of dark
  chocolate (optional)

TO SERVE (OPTIONAL)
fresh coriander (cilantro)
sour cream
guacamole
tomato salsa (see page
  253)
grated cheese
rice
tortillas

Heat the olive oil in a heavy frying pan over a high heat and brown the meat, in two or three batches. Place the meat in a casserole pot. Brown the onion in the same pan and once browned, quickly stir in the fresh chilli and garlic. Add to the meat. Add the red pepper to the pan and reduce the heat, then add the chilli powder and paprika, stirring briefly. Stir in 3–4 tbsp water and add to the casserole, then top up with just enough water to cover the meat. Cover with a lid and simmer over a low heat or in the oven at 160°C/325°F/gas 3 for 1 hour.

Stir in the cumin, tomatoes, tomato purée and beans and cook for about 30 minutes, until the beans are just soft. Season with salt to taste. Add the chocolate if using, and stir well.

Sprinkle with fresh coriander and serve with your choice of accompaniments: sour cream, guacamole, tomato salsa, grated cheese, rice and tortillas.

 See picture overleaf.

Jacob's ladder

This is another name for short ribs of beef. They can be simply braised, or you can finish them with a mouthwatering sauce, either on the barbecue or in the oven.

Braised ribs

SERVES 4

1.5 kg/3½ lb piece of short rib of beef
salt and pepper
4 carrots, sliced thickly at an angle
4 celery stalks, cut in half at an angle
2 leeks, trimmed and cut in half or thirds depending on size
1 bay leaf

Preheat the oven to 230°C/450°F/gas 8. Season the ribs and roast for 15 minutes to really brown them, then remove the meat from the roasting pan and set aside. Add the carrots, celery and leeks to the roasting pan and brown over a medium-high heat. Place the meat on top of the vegetables, add the bay leaf and pour in 300 ml/10 fl oz/1¼ cups water.

Reduce the oven temperature to 160°C/325°F/gas 3. Cover the roasting pan with foil, return to the oven and cook for 2½–3 hours, basting from time to time.

Once they are tender, you can serve the ribs with the braising juices and vegetables, or blend the braising juices and vegetables to make a hearty soup and cook the meat in a barbecue sauce.

Variation

As a variation on the simple braise, add 1 teaspoon grated fresh ginger, 2 star anise and 1 cinnamon stick (or 1 teaspoon five-spice powder), plus 2 crushed garlic cloves when browning the vegetables. Before serving, add 2–3 teaspoons soy sauce.

Barbecue sauce

1 tbsp olive oil
6 tbsp white wine vinegar
5 tbsp honey
1 tbsp tomato purée
2 tbsp passata
2 tsp whisky or Worcestershire sauce
2 tsp mustard
2 garlic cloves, crushed

Mix all the ingredients together. Cut the ribs into individual pieces and coat in the sauce. Return to the oven for 20 minutes or cook on a low barbecue.

Peanut butter sauce

5 tbsp crunchy peanut butter
55 g/2 oz/4 tbsp softened butter
grated zest and juice of 1 lime
1 tsp hot pepper jelly

Mix all the ingredients together. Cut the ribs into individual pieces and spread half the mixture over the ribs. Cook on a low barbecue for a few minutes on each side and serve with the remaining mixture.

A fresh summer grill

1 tbsp chopped fresh mint
1 tbsp chopped fresh tarragon
2 tbsp chopped chervil
1 garlic clove, crushed
1 tsp smooth English mustard
6 tbsp rapeseed oil
2 tbsp white wine vinegar
salt and pepper

Mix all the ingredients together. Cut the ribs into individual pieces and spread half the mixture over the ribs. Cook on a low barbecue for a few minutes on each side and serve with the remaining herb mixture.

Sri Lankan beef curry

Dry-roasting the spices fills the kitchen with a wonderful aroma. I suggest using a hot curry powder, as it is balanced by the coconut milk.

SERVES 4

700 g/1½ lb stewing steak, diced
1 tsp chilli powder
1 tsp medium-hot red curry powder
1 cinnamon stick
4 fresh or dried curry leaves (don't worry if you can't get them)
1 x 400 g/14 oz can coconut milk

MARINADE
1 x 400 g/14 oz can chopped tomatoes
25 g/1 oz fresh ginger, peeled
1 onion, roughly chopped
2 garlic cloves, peeled
seeds from 6 cardamom pods, crushed
pinch of salt

To make the marinade, place all the ingredients in a food processor and whizz to a rough purée. Put the beef in a glass or other non-reactive bowl, pour over the marinade and leave for a few hours or overnight.

Heat a heavy-bottomed pan over a low heat and add the chilli powder, curry powder, cinnamon and curry leaves, if using; toast for a minute or two until fragrant and beginning to darken. Add the beef and marinade, cover and simmer for 2 hours until the beef is tender.

Stir in the coconut milk and simmer, uncovered, for a further 15 minutes. Serve with rice and carrot and onion relish (see page 127).

Beef curry with spinach

Somehow the earthiness of spinach complements beef well. I often choose a spinach dish when I go to an Indian restaurant, and the classic saag gosht combines spinach and beef (or lamb) in one dish. The meat here is not marinated but is carefully mixed with the aromatic spices and then cooked with yogurt, which, with the spinach, provides the only cooking moisture.

SERVES 4–6

6 tbsp vegetable oil
4 whole black peppercorns
5 cloves
2 bay leaves
6 cardamom pods
1 onion, finely chopped
8 garlic cloves, crushed
25 g/1 oz fresh ginger,
  peeled and finely chopped
800 g/1¾ lb lean stewing
  steak, such as chuck
2 tsp cumin seeds and
  1 tsp coriander seeds,
  ground together in a
  pestle and mortar
¼ tsp cayenne pepper
2 tsp salt
5 tbsp plain yogurt
800 g/1¾ lb fresh spinach,
  washed thoroughly and
  finely chopped
2 pinches of garam masala

Heat a large, heavy-bottomed pan over a medium heat, add the oil and then stir in the peppercorns, cloves, bay leaves and cardamoms. Stir for a moment or two to warm the spices. Add the onion, garlic and ginger and stir until the onion starts to colour. Lower the heat and add the meat, the cumin, coriander, cayenne and salt and stir to combine really well.

Stir in the yogurt a spoonful at a time, then add the spinach and mix thoroughly until the spinach wilts. Cover with a tight-fitting lid and simmer over a very low heat for about 2 hours. There should be enough moisture, but if you think it is getting dry add a little water – the secret is to not have too high a heat.

Stir in the garam masala and cook over a medium-low heat for 5 minutes. Serve with rice and tomato and coriander salad (see page 127). Avoid eating the peppercorns, cloves and cardamoms!

SPICE OF LIFE

Whenever you serve curry, a selection of homemade side dishes – along with a few good chutneys and pickles – makes a real feast. All these recipes serve four.

Onion relish

1 onion, peeled
1/2 tsp salt
4 tsp lemon juice
1/4 tsp paprika
pinch of cayenne

Cut the onion in half from top to bottom and then slice thinly across the grain. Mix in a bowl with all the other ingredients, and leave for at least 30 minutes to allow the flavours to develop.

Cucumber & yogurt raita

1/4 cucumber
1 shallot, finely chopped
1 tsp salt
1 tomato, blanched, peeled and diced
1/2 tbsp chopped fresh mint
1/2 tbsp chopped fresh parsley
150 g/5 1/2 oz/generous 1/2 cup plain yogurt
1/2 tsp cumin seeds, lightly crushed and toasted

Cut the cucumber in half lengthways, discard the seeds and cut the flesh into dice. Mix with the shallot and salt and leave for 10 minutes. Squeeze out the liquid and gently mix with the other ingredients. Season and chill.

Dal

1/2 tsp cumin seeds
4 tbsp vegetable oil
2–3 shallots, finely chopped
3 garlic cloves, crushed
200 g/7 oz green lentils, rinsed
1/2 tsp salt
pinch of cayenne pepper

Place a heavy-bottomed pan over a medium heat and toast the cumin seeds gently, stirring frequently, for 2–3 minutes, until fragrant. Reduce the heat, add the oil and the shallots and cook until softened and lightly coloured.

Stir in the garlic, followed by the lentils, stir to coat and then pour in 700 ml/1 1/2 pints/3 cups water. Bring to the boil, cover and reduce the heat to a very gentle simmer. Cook for about 1 1/4 hours, adding a little more water if the lentils seem to be getting dry. When the lentils are soft, add the salt and cayenne, simmer for a minute or two, then serve.

Carrot & onion relish

225 g/8 oz carrots, finely grated
1 onion, finely chopped
$1/2$ tsp salt
black pepper
juice of 1 lemon
pinch of cayenne
$1/2$ tsp grated fresh ginger
$1/2$ tsp black mustard seeds

Gently mix all the ingredients together and leave for 30 minutes to allow the flavours to develop.

Tomato & coriander salad

225 g/8 oz tomatoes, blanched and peeled
2 shallots, finely chopped
1 tbsp rapeseed oil
salt and pepper
4 tbsp chopped fresh coriander (cilantro)
$1/2$ tsp toasted cumin seeds

Slice the tomatoes thinly and spread over a flat dish. Sprinkle the shallots and oil over the tomatoes, season with salt and pepper and then sprinkle over the coriander and cumin seeds. Leave for at least 30 minutes to allow the flavours to develop.

Cardamom basmati rice

325 g/$11^1/2$ oz/$1^3/4$ cups basmati rice
$1/2$ tsp salt
20 cardamom pods, lightly crushed
15 g/$1/2$ oz/1 tbsp butter

Rinse the rice in cold water, drain and place in a bowl, then pour 1.2 litres/2 pints/5 cups cold water over it and leave to soak for 30 minutes.

Drain and put the rice in a pan with 570 ml/20 fl oz/scant $2^1/2$ cups water, salt, cardamoms and butter. Bring to the boil and cover with a tight-fitting lid, turn the heat to very low and cook for 20 minutes.

Mix very gently with a carving fork, then replace the lid and leave to stand for 5 minutes. Before serving, fluff up with the carving fork.

Beef olives with lemon & herbs

This dish has a long history – and there are no olives in it! Stuffings are an economical way of making good-quality beef go further and I love experimenting with this idea. You can make a meaty stuffing using leftovers or trimmings or some chopped bacon. This version is stuffed with herby lemony breadcrumbs and makes a delicious supper dish. Ask your butcher to cut the beef into thin, even slices.

SERVES 4

12 thin slices of raw lean
  beef, such as topside
  (top round)
125 g/4^{1}/2 oz/2 cups fresh
  breadcrumbs
1 onion, finely chopped
grated zest o f 1 lemon
1 tbsp fresh chopped
  parsley and marjoram
2 egg yolks
salt and pepper
3 tbsp seasoned flour
2 tbsp vegetable oil
600 ml/20 fl oz/2^{1}/2 cups
  beef stock

Trim the beef slices of any fat or gristle and cut into 15 x 10 cm/6 x 4 in pieces. Place the slices of meat between two sheets of clingfilm (plastic wrap) and beat with a rolling pin to flatten them as thinly as you can, being careful not to tear them.

Mix the breadcrumbs with the onion, lemon zest, herbs and egg yolks and season well. Spread a tablespoon of the mixture on each piece of meat, roll up and secure with a cocktail stick or string.

Preheat the oven to 160°C/325°F/gas 3. Lightly coat the beef rolls in seasoned flour. Heat a large ovenproof pan over a high heat, add the oil and quickly brown the beef all over. Add the stock, cover with a well-fitting lid and cook for about 1–1^{1}/2 hours or until the meat is tender. Serve with mashed potatoes and green vegetables.

📷 See picture opposite and overleaf.

Larks and beef birds

The name 'olives' derives from the Old French *alou*, meaning lark (the modern French word is *alouette*) – because the rolled-up beef resembles small birds prepared for the table. This may seem far-fetched today, but small birds often appeared on medieval tables: in 1378 the price of food sold by London's public cookshops was subject to regulation, and included the following: five roast larks, 1½d; three roast thrushes, 2d; ten roast finches, 1d – or you could get a roast hen for 4d. As late as 1788 Richard Briggs was serving roasted larks in his London tavern.

Beef, veal or mutton were rolled and filled with various stuffings to make birds, or olives, and Gervase Markham in *The English Housewife* (1615) gives a recipe for Olive pie, in which thin slices of veal are rolled around a mixture of herbs (including violet leaves, spinach, sorrel, thyme and scallions), egg yolks, currants and spices, then covered with butter and baked in a pie.

Toad in the hole

I don't know who first coined the phrase 'toad in the hole' for this classic British supper dish. Historically, cooking in batter seems to have been a way to make bits of meat go further. In the eighteenth century it was an inexpensive dish (if you happened to have a dovecote) made with squabs, or young pigeons; Elizabeth Raffald's *The Experienced English Housekeeper* (1769) was one of several cookbooks that included 'pigeons in a hole'. A recipe for 'toad in a hole' appeared in *The English Art of Cookery* (1788) by Richard Briggs, a cook in London taverns. His recipe calls for a 'veiney piece of beef', which is baked in batter for 2 hours. Other toads in the hole were made with lamb chops, fillet and sirloin steaks, or leftover stewed beef. However, some references imply a certain aversion to putting the noble sirloin into a batter pudding, which I endorse (the very idea!). Mrs Beeton's recipe in *The Book of Household Management* (1861) uses rump steak and sheep's kidney, but she also suggested that 'the remains of cold beef, rather underdone, may be substituted for the steak'. Sausages are the usual 'toads' in today's versions, although I have seen a recipe from the 1930s that uses tomatoes.

My recipe calls for the very best beef sausages, which are first browned in the pan, then the batter is poured over them into the hot fat. In a hot oven, the batter rises around the sausages — or toads, if you like.

SERVES 4

2 eggs
115 g/4 oz/1 cup plain
  (all-purpose) flour
200 ml/7 fl oz/generous
  ³/4 cup full-fat milk
100 ml/3¹/2 fl oz/6–7 tbsp
  water
salt
about 3 tbsp dripping
450 g/1 lb good-quality
  beef sausages

Put the eggs into a food processor, followed by the flour and then the milk, water and salt. Whizz until well combined, scrape the sides of the processor with a spatula and whizz again. Strain into a jug and leave to rest for 20 minutes.

Preheat the oven to 200°C/400°F/gas 6. Heat the dripping in a roasting pan over a medium heat, and brown the sausages in the dripping. When the oven is hot, pour the batter over the sausages and bake for 30 minutes. The batter should be well risen and brown, with the sausages peeping through.

Onion gravy

I like to serve onion gravy with Toad in the hole. This also goes extremely well with calves' liver. I usually add a splash of balsamic vinegar, or Marsala wine, just before serving, too.

SERVES 4

8 onions
2 tbsp water
1 tsp sugar
600 ml/20 fl oz/2½ cups
  beef stock
salt and pepper

Slice the onions thinly. The best way to do this is to peel them, then cut them in half lengthways, place on a board, cut side down, and cut off the hard root and then slice along the grain.

Put the onions in a heavy-bottomed pan with the water and sugar and cook very slowly, stirring from time to time until they soften and begin to caramelize. If you have good firm onions, you may not need the sugar, but some onions can be watery and the sugar helps to caramelize them. Leave them over a low heat, stirring occasionally, until they are really softened and browned; this may take 30 minutes to 1 hour.

Add the stock and reduce to a lovely rich sauce. Season. This will keep in the fridge for up to three days and it improves with keeping.

PIES & PUDDINGS

The pies that graced the banquets of medieval and Renaissance Europe were elaborately decorated with patterned pastry trimmings in different colours — sometimes even gilded. 'Great pies' contained beef and assorted domestic poultry and wild birds, together with spices and currants. Elizabethan 'minced pies' were made of shredded beef, veal or mutton with chopped suet and dried fruits such as raisins and prunes, flavoured with orange, lemon, rosewater and spices. Over the centuries the meat content was gradually reduced, and today the mince pies we enjoy at Christmas are entirely meat-free.

A pie dish can be any shape or size, but ideally it should have a wide rim to support the pastry lid. For larger pies, or those with a long cooking time, it is useful to support the pastry in the centre with a pie funnel: this also allows steam to escape, so the pastry doesn't get soggy. Traditional English pie funnels are made in the shape of small blackbirds. It's also traditional to decorate savoury pies with pastry trimmings — from simple leaf shapes to elaborate patterns of shapes, leaves and flowers.

Puddings were originally mixtures of breadcrumbs, suet and other ingredients, both sweet and savoury, boiled in animal guts — still used for the French *boudin*, or blood pudding. In the early seventeenth century pudding cloths replaced the guts, making them both more convenient and more versatile: the English became famous for the variety of their puddings. The savoury suet pudding is just one branch of the pudding family tree, based on a suet pastry that is boiled or steamed so it remains moist.

Steaming

If you have a steamer, great. If not, you'll need a pan large enough and deep enough to hold the pudding bowl. Place an upside-down lid or trivet in the pan so the pudding is raised above the bottom of the pan. Put the pudding onto the trivet and half-fill the pan with boiling water. Lower the heat to a gentle simmer, cover the pan and steam. Alternatively, place in the simmering oven of an Aga.

Steak & kidney pudding

My wife makes a glorious pud and her recipe has been honed over the years – nothing fancy, as you shouldn't mess too much with classics. She includes dried herbs in the suet crust, which the purist in me objected to, but herbes de Provence are very good. The beauty of this dish is that it will sit happily for half an hour or so until you want it, so if guests are late or that extra glass of wine takes a little longer, lunch can wait.

SERVES 6

450 g/1 lb stewing steak, trimmed and diced
125 g/4½ oz ox kidney, trimmed and diced
1–2 tbsp seasoned flour
1 onion, chopped
100 g/3½ oz button mushrooms, quartered
1 tbsp chopped fresh parsley
100 ml/3½ fl oz/6–7 tbsp red wine
stock or water

SUET CRUST
280 g/10 oz/2¼ cups self-raising flour
pinch of salt
140 g/5 oz shredded suet
1 tsp dried herbes de Provence

To make the suet crust, sift the flour and salt together into a bowl, stir in the suet and herbs, then add 150–200ml/5–7 fl oz/about ¾ cup cold water to form a pliable dough that comes away from the sides of the bowl.

Grease a 1.2 litre/2 pint/5 cup pudding bowl and measure it from rim to rim, going underneath the bowl. On a lightly floured surface, roll out the pastry to a circle of the measured diameter; cut out a quarter segment and set aside for the lid. Lift the pastry into the bowl, pressing the two cut edges together to seal. Leave any pastry that's hanging over the rim. Roll out the reserved segment of pastry to make a pastry lid.

Toss the steak and kidney in the seasoned flour, then mix with the onion, mushrooms and parsley. Place in the pudding bowl and add the red wine; top up to two-thirds full with stock or water. Dampen the pastry edges and place the pastry lid on top, trim and pinch the edges together to seal.

Cover the pudding with greaseproof (wax) paper, with a pleat to allow for expansion. For extra peace of mind, cover the paper with foil, similarly pleated, and tie a piece of string round the rim to hold them in place. It's also useful to make a string 'handle' to help remove the pudding when cooked, because when it's hot it's hard to get a grip! Steam for 4 hours.

Steak & oyster pie

These days oysters are often thought of as something of an acquired taste, not to mention an extravagance, but for hundreds of years they were food for the poor in many coastal areas of Britain. Beefsteak and oyster pie has a far longer history than steak and kidney. Musselburgh, east of Edinburgh, was famous for its mussel and oyster beds, and Musselburgh pie is a local name for this dish.

SERVES 6

1 kg/2¹/₄ lb rump steak, cut into 12 very thin slices
6 slices of unsmoked streaky bacon
12 oysters, freshly shucked
plain flour seasoned with salt, pepper and cayenne pepper
5 shallots, finely chopped
1 tbsp chopped fresh parsley
300 ml/10 fl oz/1¹/₄ cups beef stock
450 g/1 lb puff pastry
1 egg, beaten

Place each slice of steak between two sheets of clingfilm (plastic wrap) and beat out, using a rolling pin, until the pieces measure about 10 x 5 cm/4 x 2 in.

Cut the bacon slices in half lengthways and roll each piece around an oyster. Then turn the rolled-up bacon through 90 degrees and roll up in the pieces of steak, so that the oysters won't slip out. Roll in the seasoned flour and place in a 1.5 litre/2½ pint/6½ cup pie dish. Sprinkle with the shallots and parsley and pour in the stock.

Roll out the pastry, dampen the rim of the pie dish and roll the pastry over the pie, pressing down to seal around the rim. Make a hole in the centre of the pastry, then brush with beaten egg. If you like, decorate with shapes cut from the pastry trimmings, brushing these lightly with egg. Leave to rest in a cool place for 30 minutes.

Preheat the oven to 220°C/425°F/gas 7. Cook the pie for 15 minutes, then reduce the oven temperature to 180°C/350°F/gas 4 and cook for a further 45 minutes to 1 hour. Check after about 30 minutes, and if the pastry is getting too brown, cover with foil.

Variations

Instead of slicing the steak, cut it into 2 cm/¾ in cubes. Chop the bacon.

Beef, chorizo and red pepper

Omit the bacon and oysters. Sauté 1 or 2 roughly chopped red peppers with 1 chopped garlic clove and 50 g/1¾ oz diced chorizo.

Beef and mushroom

Omit the oysters. Use fresh thyme leaves instead of parsley. Briefly sauté 400g/14 oz quartered fresh mushrooms and add with the shallots.

Steak and ale

Omit the oysters. Use ale or Guiness/stout instead of stock.

Steak and Stilton

Omit the bacon and oysters. Add 100 g/3½ oz crumbled Stilton with the shallots and parsley.

Rump steak
& game pie

This recipe is based on one by the late Michael Smith, but over the years I've
reworked and developed it. It's a versatile recipe for the autumn and winter: you
can use almost any game, such as wild duck, pigeon, pieces of hare or wild rabbit,
or odd bits of venison. I always use rump steak as the base for this pie because it
gives it a richness that might otherwise be missing. If you have a big pot and a
couple of large pie dishes, it's easy to double up the recipe — or you can make one
pie and a casserole to freeze for later.

SERVES 6

1 pheasant or grouse,
  2 partridge – or other
  game birds, ideally with
  their livers; older birds
  are preferable
2 tbsp olive oil
½ a hare, 1 wild rabbit or
  about 400 g/14 oz venison
500 g/1 lb 2 oz rump steak,
  trimmed of all fat and cut
  into approximately 3
  cm/1¼ in cubes
70 g/2½ oz/5 tbsp butter
1 large onion, sliced
225 g/8 oz button
  mushrooms, cut into
  quarters
2 garlic cloves, crushed
40 g/1½ oz/5 tbsp plain
  (all-purpose) flour
salt and pepper
2 tbsp tomato purée
4 whole cloves
2 bay leaves
5 sage leaves
juice and grated zest
  of 1 orange
2 tbsp rowan or redcurrant
  jelly
1 bottle red wine
400 g/14 oz puff pastry

Wipe the game birds dry with kitchen paper. Heat half the oil in a heavy-bottomed pan and brown the birds on all sides; remove and put into a large, deep casserole. Brown the pieces of hare in the same way. Add the remaining olive oil to the pan and brown the steak, then tip into the casserole, along with any juices.

Preheat the oven to 160°C/325°F/gas 3. Melt 55 g/2 oz butter in the pan and brown the onion, then add the mushrooms and garlic. Stir in the flour and season. Add the tomato purée, cloves, bay and sage, orange zest and juice, rowan jelly and red wine and bring to the boil. Simmer gently for a minute, scraping any residue off the bottom of the pan, then pour it over the meat in the casserole. Add a little water if necessary, to cover the birds. Cover with a lid and cook in the oven for about 2–2½ hours, or until the birds and hare are tender.

Remove the birds and hare, then set aside until cool enough to handle. Remove the skin and discard. Take the meat off the bones and cut into chunks, slightly larger than the rump steak, return to the casserole.

If you have the birds' livers, cut them into small dice, quickly fry them in the remaining butter and add to the casserole. Simmer for a further 2 minutes and then check the seasoning and consistency: if it is too thin, simmer gently to reduce slightly.

Leave to cool and then place all the meat and sauce in a large, deep pie dish. Roll out the pastry, dampen the rim of the pie dish and roll the pastry over the pie, pressing down to seal around the rim. Make a hole in the centre of the pastry, then brush with beaten egg. If you like, decorate with shapes cut from the pastry trimmings, brushing these lightly with egg. Leave to rest in a cool place for 30 minutes.

Preheat the oven to 220°C/425°F/gas 7. Cook the pie for 15 minutes, then reduce the oven temperature to 180°C/350°F/gas 4 and cook for a further 30 minutes.

Pasties

The original packed lunch! A pasty is an old English word for a pie of meat baked without a dish. One story has it that the famous Cornish variety used the pastry wrapping in order that the poisons from the tin mines didn't get into the meat – the pastry edges were not eaten but simply used to hold the filling. In Scotland, the horseshoe-shaped Forfar bridie is a good luck symbol for the bride, eaten at the wedding breakfast. To avoid bruising local pride, I have just called this a pasty.

MAKES 10

900 g/2 lb/7¼ cups plain (all-purpose) flour
1 tsp salt
225 g/8 oz/1 cup butter, diced
225 g/8 oz/1 cup lard, diced
1 egg, beaten with 1 tbsp cold water

FILLING
1.2 kg/2½ lb rump steak
150 g/5½ oz fresh beef suet
4 onions, finely chopped
salt and pepper

First, make the pastry: put the flour and salt in a food processor, then add the butter and lard and whizz until the mixture resembles fine breadcrumbs. Pour in about 6 tbsp of cold water and whizz to form a dough, adding more cold water if needed – do not overprocess. Wrap in clingfilm (plastic wrap) and leave to rest in the fridge for 30 minutes.

To make the filling, trim the meat of any excess fat and cut into 1 cm/½ in chunks. Chop the suet finely and mix with the meat and onions. Season well.

Preheat the oven to 200°C/400°F/gas 6. Line a large baking sheet with baking parchment.

Divide the pastry into 10 pieces and roll out, not too thinly, into 18 cm/7 in rounds. Divide the meat mixture among them. Dampen the pastry edges with cold water and fold the pastry over the filling. Press together and use a fork to crimp the edges to seal securely. Make a small hole in the top of each pasty and brush with beaten egg.

Place the pasties on the baking sheet and bake for 45–50 minutes, until golden brown. Serve hot or cold.

Tips

- Ask your butcher for a piece of fresh beef suet. Don't be tempted to use the flour-coated, ready-made shredded suet.

- I based this on the Scottish version, just meat and onion, but if you like, you can replace some of the meat or onion with finely diced potato or carrot.

See picture overleaf for filling the individual pasties.

THE HUMBLE PASTY

It's a bit of a mystery why pasties have become so closely linked with Cornwall, since the origins of the pasty are buried in history. The English word 'pasty' comes from the Old French *paste*, which in turn came from the Latin *pasta*, meaning paste or dough. One of the earliest known European cookery manuscripts, dating from around 1300, in Danish with Latin recipe headings, describes how to make a *pastellum*, or pasty, of deer marrow. In London, a list of cookshop prices in 1378 includes 'capon baked in a pasty, 8d'. *Le Ménagier de Paris*, a book written in 1393 for a young French housewife, gives recipes for venison, beef, mutton and veal pasties. In the Middle Ages the term seems to apply to a baked pastry case containing a single main ingredient – meat, poultry or fish – whereas a pie held a variety of fillings.

Venison pasties are prominent in the literature of the sixteenth and seventeenth centuries, when venison was the preserve of the wealthy – but so was much of the literature. It is likely that poorer families made pasties with root vegetables and onions, but simply didn't write about them.

Samuel Pepys seems to have been exceptionally fond of venison pasties, mentioning them around fifty times in his diaries in the 1660s.

Laura Mason and Catherine Brown, authors of *The Taste of Britain*, believe that the use of the word 'pasty' declined during the eighteenth century, except in Cornwall, where it remained the lunch of choice for the tin miners. Pasties were easy to carry and the pastry protected the contents. Curiously, fishermen believed that it was unlucky to take a pasty on a boat.

In 2011 the Cornish pasty was awarded Protected Geographical Indication (PGI) status, which means that only Cornish pasties prepared in Cornwall and following the traditional recipe can be called 'Cornish pasties'. The Cornish Pasty Association says that an authentic Cornish pasty has a distinctive 'D' shape and is crimped on one side, never on top. (Many Cornish bakers argue this point, saying that the top crimp has been traditional for generations.) The filling consists of uncooked minced or roughly cut chunks of beef (not less than 12.5%), swede, potato and onion, with a light peppery seasoning.

A Scottish version of the pasty, the Forfar bridie, is filled with chopped beef and onions. Cornish miners took their pasties to the United States, and the pasty has become particularly associated with the copper mining communities in Michigan.

All over the world you will find variations of this perfectly portable pie, including Jamaica's spicy beef patties, the *pastes* found in the state of Hidalgo in Mexico, and Argentina's *empanadas*.

Ragù

This basic Italian sauce can be made with beef or veal or a mixture of the two. Serve it with pasta or use it to stuff peppers or a marrow before baking them in the oven. It is also the basis for lasagne.

SERVES 4, WITH PASTA

2 tbsp olive oil
1 onion, chopped finely
1 large carrot, chopped finely
1 celery stalk, chopped finely
2 garlic cloves, chopped
250 g/9 oz minced (ground) beef or veal
3 chicken livers, chopped in small pieces
3 large ripe tomatoes, blanched, peeled and chopped
sprig of thyme
salt and pepper
125 ml/4 fl oz/½ cup red wine
200 ml/7 fl oz/generous ¾ cup stock
2 tbsp double (heavy) cream

Heat the olive oil in a heavy-bottomed pan over a medium heat and cook the chopped vegetables until soft. Add the garlic, stir briefly, then add the meat and livers and stir well until they just lose their raw look. Add the tomatoes and thyme and cook gently for a few minutes, seasoning with salt and pepper.

Add the wine and allow to reduce slowly for about 15 minutes. Add the stock and continue to simmer over a very low heat, uncovered, for a further 1–1½ hours, adding a little water if the sauce looks dry. Stir in the cream and remove from the heat.

Lasagne

I can remember making this once a week as a 'special' at the Savoy. Our ragù sauce had cooked for hours until it was beautifully creamy. We all hoped that the dish wouldn't sell because then we could feast on the lasagne for our own lunch. In those days we had to cook the pasta sheets first in boiling water and then refresh them before layering with the meat sauce and béchamel. Nowadays you can use fresh pasta or no-cook pasta. As well as a rich ragù, you need a well-flavoured béchamel sauce.

SERVES 8

1–2 tbsp olive oil
400 g/14 oz fresh or
  no-cook lasagne sheets
ragù (see opposite)
Parmesan cheese, grated

BÉCHAMEL SAUCE
900 ml/30 fl oz/3¾ cups
  full-fat milk
1 onion, studded with
  4 cloves
1 bay leaf
6 peppercorns
sprigs of parsley and thyme
85 g/3 oz/6 tbsp butter
85 g/3 oz/scant ¾ cup
  plain (all-purpose) flour
salt and pepper

To make the béchamel sauce, put the milk in a pan with the onion, bay leaf, peppercorns, parsley and thyme. Bring just to the boil, then remove from the heat and leave for at least 10 minutes to infuse the flavours. Strain into a jug.

Melt the butter over a low heat in a heavy-bottomed pan. Add the flour and stir continuously with a wooden spoon for about 2 minutes. Gradually add the hot milk, beating continuously until smooth. Continue to cook for a further 4–5 minutes until smooth and creamy. Season to taste.

Preheat the oven to 200°C/400°F/gas 6. Lightly oil a large ovenproof dish or roasting pan. Line the pan with lasagne, cutting the sheets to fit as necessary; don't overlap the pieces by more than about 5 mm/¼ in and don't have pasta going up the sides of the dish. Cover with a thin layer of ragù, then a layer of béchamel sauce. Repeat the layers of pasta, ragù and béchamel. Sprinkle with cheese and bake for 25–30 minutes, until golden and browned in places. Leave to stand for 5 minutes before serving.

Pastitsio

A variation of lasagne from Greece; my wife used to make this for our children. You can add a teaspoon of ground cinnamon to the ragù for an authentic touch.

SERVES 8

400 g/14 oz dried macaroni
salt and pepper
ragù (see page 148)
béchamel sauce (see page 149)
Parmesan or pecorino cheese, grated

Preheat the oven to 180°C/350°F/gas 4. Cook the macaroni in boiling water until al dente, refresh under cold water and drain well. Spread half in a large ovenproof dish or roasting pan. Season and cover with the ragù, then add another layer of macaroni and cover with the béchamel. Sprinkle on lots of grated Parmesan and bake for 45–50 minutes until browned and bubbling. Serve with a green salad, for example romaine lettuce.

Meatloaf

Simple, no-fuss food for a weekday supper or served cold for a picnic.

SERVES 6–8

2 tbsp butter
2 onions, finely chopped
1 garlic clove, crushed
900 g/2 lb minced
  (ground) beef
about 140 g/5 oz/3 cups
  fresh breadcrumbs
2 tbsp chopped fresh
  oregano, or 1 tbsp
  dried oregano
1 tsp ground mace
1 tsp paprika
1½ tsp salt
1½ tsp pepper
2 eggs, beaten
5–6 thin slice of unsmoked
  streaky bacon
tomato sauce (see opposite
  page), to serve

Preheat the oven to 190°C/375°F/gas 5. Heat the butter in a frying pan, add the onions and cook gently for 10–15 minutes until softened and golden. Add the garlic, stir for a few moments, then tip into a large bowl.

Add the beef, breadcrumbs, oregano, spices, salt and pepper and work everything together until evenly combined – it's easiest to do this using your hands. Add the eggs and mix well.

Line a deep 900 g/2 lb loaf tin with the bacon, then press the beef mixture into the tin and bake for about 50–60 minutes, until cooked through (test with a skewer). Leave in the tin for 5 minutes, then turn out, slice and serve hot with tomato sauce.

To serve cold, cover with foil and add a couple of weights (or cans of food) and leave until cold, then refrigerate.

Tips

- Oregano is particularly good if you're serving this with tomato sauce, but you could use another herb instead: marjoram, parsley or thyme, for example. Or you could add a dash of Worcestershire or Tabasco sauce.

- Try serving with onion gravy (page 133) instead of tomato sauce.

Tomato sauce

Every cook has their own tomato sauce recipe, and this is mine. It has developed over the years from my days in the kitchens of the Savoy hotel, London, whose original chef was Auguste Escoffier and who in the 1870s came up with the idea of canning tomatoes. You can use fresh tomatoes if you can get really ripe ones, or canned ones will do.

**MAKES ABOUT
850 ML/1½ PINTS/
3½ CUPS**

2 tbsp olive oil
1 large onion, chopped
1 celery stalk, chopped
1 carrot, chopped
1 kg/2¼ lb fresh ripe
  tomatoes, roughly
  chopped, or 800 g/
  1lb 12 oz canned
  chopped plum tomatoes
1 garlic clove, crushed
1 bay leaf
1 sprig of thyme
1 strip of orange peel
salt and pepper

Heat the olive oil in a heavy-bottomed pan, then gently cook the onion, celery and carrot until softened but not coloured, about 15 minutes.

Add the tomatoes plus a can full of water, or 125 ml/4 fl oz/½ cup water if cooking fresh tomatoes. Reduce the heat to a very gentle simmer, add the garlic, herbs, orange peel and seasoning and cook very gently for 30 minutes, adding a little more water if it seems to be getting dry.

You can either push this sauce through a sieve or liquidize it first and then sieve it, which makes sieving easier. But it must be sieved to remove the pips and herby bits. This will keep, covered, in the fridge for a week.

Moroccan meatballs with lemon sauce

This Moroccan-style stew uses ras el hanout, a spice mix that translates as 'top of the shop' – in other words, the spice merchant's best mix. It's easy to find ras el hanout in shops, supermarkets or online.

SERVES 4

1 onion, roughly chopped
2 tbsp picked coriander leaves
2 slices of 2- or 3-day-old brown bread, crusts removed
500 g/1 lb 2 oz minced (ground) beef (10–15% fat)
1 egg
2 tsp ras el hanout
salt and pepper

LEMON SAUCE
1 tbsp vegetable oil
1 onion, finely chopped
$^1/_2$ tsp paprika
1 tsp turmeric
1 tsp ground cumin
1 garlic clove, crushed
350 ml/12 fl oz/1$^1/_2$ cups stock or water
2 tbsp lemon juice
4 tbsp chopped flat-leaf parsley

You can chop the onion and coriander by hand or do it in a food processor. If the latter, you can add the bread after they have been processed a little; otherwise, just rub or grate the bread to form rough crumbs.

Mix the bread and onion mixture with the meat, egg, ras el hanout, salt and pepper until everything is evenly blended. Shape into 20–24 small balls – the size of large walnuts – and place on a tray, cover with clingfilm (plastic wrap) and chill.

To make the sauce, heat the oil in a wide pan, add the onion and soften for about 5 minutes. Stir in the paprika, turmeric and cumin and cook for a further minute. Add the garlic, stir for a few moments and then add the stock. Place the meatballs into the sauce, give them a gentle shake and then cover the pan and cook over a low heat for 40 minutes.

To finish, stir in the lemon juice and chopped parsley and reduce, uncovered, over a medium heat until it thickens slightly. Serve with rice or couscous.

Tip

For a slightly richer sauce, mix the lemon juice with 2 egg yolks in a small bowl, then whisk in 4 tbsp of the cooking liquid. Stir into the pan, together with the parsley, and heat very gently until slightly thickened.

Preserved beef

Before the advent of refrigeration, there were two options when it came to killing a cow (or a pig) for its meat: feast on the fresh meat or preserve it to provide food for months to come. Feasting, for the majority of people, meant a special occasion or religious festival; preserving was the practical solution. For thousands of years the most reliable way to preserve food was by salting. In the early Iron Age the Austrian village now known as Hallstatt – from *hals*, Greek for salt – became rich through its salt mines, trading across Europe in salt and salted pork and beef. A twelfth-century Irish legend *Aislinge meic Con Glinne*, the Vision of MacConglinne, includes several references to corned (salted) beef among the descriptions of an imaginary land made of food.

Salt acts as a preservative by drawing out moisture: this stops bacteria and moulds from growing because they need water to survive. There are two main methods of salting: rubbing with dry salt or soaking in brine, either of which may take a few days or several weeks. The salt-cured meat may then be hung up to dry, either in fresh air (only possible in dry climates) or in smoke, which adds to the flavour – for better or for worse! Wet-cured or brined meat is sometimes referred to as 'pickled'. The distinction was made between 'green' beef – salted overnight for short-term keeping, much as today we brine meat mainly to heighten the flavour – and 'hung' beef, which was smoked for longer keeping.

Throughout western Europe the feast day of St Martin, or Martinmas, was celebrated on 11 November; the feast was often followed by a period of fasting, as families prepared themselves for several months of scarcity. Cattle and pigs were slaughtered for the Martinmas feast, but most of their meat was preserved as provision for the months ahead. The British Isles have always been renowned for beef, and references to 'Martlemas' beef go back at least 700 years. *The Englishman's Food* (Drummond and Wilbraham) cites a manor in the reign of Edward II where the larder held '600 bacons, 80 carcasses of martilmasse beef and 600 muttons'.

To have Martlemas beef implied a well-stocked larder. The autumn slaughter also saved the expense of feeding cattle through the winter on dried peas, hay and straw, as the English farmer-poet Thomas Tusser noted in 1557:

> *For Easter, at Martilmas, hang up a beef,*
> *For pease fed and stall fed play pickpurse the thief.*
> *With that and fat bacon, till grass beef come in,*
> *Thy folk shall look cheerly, when others look thin.*

The salted Martlemas beef was often hung in the chimney to dry (as was bacon), and to some people the word evoked an image of overly smoky and dried-out meat: Andrew Boorde (c.1490–1549) wrote 'Martlemas beef, which is called hanged beef, in the roof of the smoky house is not laudable.' Later, the inclusion of sugar in the salt cure seems to have given a better result. Eliza Smith's *The Compleat Housewife* (first published in 1727) gives a method for Dutch beef, prepared with brown sugar, salt and saltpetre and hung to dry in a chimney. F Marian McNeill's fascinating book *The Scots Kitchen* (1929) gives an early nineteenth-century recipe for Beef-Ham: a twenty-pound rump is rubbed with a mixture of salt, saltpetre, raw sugar, cloves, Jamaica pepper (allspice) and black pepper, then marinated for three weeks, being turned every other day. The drained meat is boiled or baked, or could also be smoked – hung over a barrel 'in which you burn peat or turf'.

Of course, beef didn't have to be smoked after salting. Scottish author Martin Martin in *A Description of the Western Isles* (1703) wrote 'The natives are accustomed to salt their Beef in a Cow's Hide, which keeps it close from Air and preserves it as well, if not better than Barrels...This Beef is transported to Glasgow, a city in the West of Scotland, and from thence, being put into Barrels, exported to the Indies in good Condition.'

For long-distance sea journeys, salt or 'barrel' beef and pork were an inevitable part of sailors' diets. British Navy regulations in 1565 stipulated that each sailor receive a weekly ration of seven gallons of beer, eight pounds of salt beef, seven pounds of biscuit (dried bread), three-quarters of a pound of stock fish, plus butter and cheese. To ensure that it would keep for many months, the meat had to be heavily salted. Consequently it needed lengthy soaking before cooking – when the ship's cook failed to soak the meat properly, it would have been pretty unpalatable.

For 200 years, from the mid-1600s to the nineteenth century, Ireland cornered the world market in corned beef. Based on an established trade in salt with France and beef from its green pastures, Irish salt beef was exported to sugar plantations in the West Indies and to cities in Europe and North America. Cork, in the south of Ireland, where ships stopped for provisions before crossing the Atlantic, gained an advantage over its competitors in the cured beef trade, Belfast and Dublin. Wealthy Cork city dwellers enjoyed the prime cuts that were not needed for salting, while slaughterhouse employees were given a weekly allowance of fresh offal. The blood went to make drisheen, a black pudding that is still a speciality of Cork.

Many people associate salt beef with Jewish cooking, and this is nothing new. In *The Art of Cookery made Plain and Easy* (1747), Hannah Glasse gives a recipe for 'the Jews way to pickle beef, which will go good to the West Indies, and keep a year good in the pickle, and with care will go to the East Indies.' The Ashkenazi Jews of Europe developed their own cuisine based on Kosher dietary laws, which decreed that only the forequarters of the beast were eaten (the hindquarters, which yield tender cuts such as sirloin, were forbidden); the meat also had to be prepared within 72 hours of slaughter. In order to keep a supply of beef it had to be preserved by salting, and without time to hang and tenderize, long, slow cooking was required until the meat was very tender.

Corned beef and the modern English term 'salt beef' are interchangeable, 'corn' being an old English word for any grain, including grains of salt. The classic recipe uses brisket or silverside (outside or bottom round), kept in a spiced brine for up to two weeks. The resulting meat is usually gently simmered with onions, carrots and bay leaves, until tender enough to cut with a fork. It's the basis for the traditional English 'boiled beef and carrots', North America's New England boiled dinner and the Irish-American corned beef and cabbage.

Nowadays, when people in Britain talk about corned beef they usually mean the chopped, pressed meat sold in distinctive oblong tins. Beef processing plants established in South America in the late nineteenth century created a cheap, more consistent and easily transportable form of preserved beef – just in time to feed the British armed forces in the First and Second World Wars. The servicemen gave it the nickname 'bully beef', a corruption of the French *bouilli*, meaning boiled. It was finally dropped from the troops' ration packs in 2009, but dishes such as corned beef hash – diced meat fried with onions and diced boiled potatoes and topped with a poached egg – retain a nostalgic appeal, for some people at least.

Pastrami starts out like corned (salt) beef: a brisket soaked in brine. After brining it is coated in crushed peppercorns and other spices, which can include garlic, coriander, paprika, cloves, allspice and mustard seeds, and then smoked. The recipe, an adaptation of the Balkan pastirma (see page 161), was brought to the US by Jews from Eastern and Central Europe.

In the classic New York pastrami on rye sandwich, the pastrami is served hot from a steamer, sliced thinly, piled onto rye bread and served with pickles.

Spiced beef evolved from salt beef. A piece of beef (usually round, topside or brisket) is dry-salted with various spices, garlic, sugar or black treacle, and then either smoked or gently simmered; it is usually pressed and served cold, carved in thin slices, although it may be served hot. Spiced beef was once popular throughout England and Ireland, especially at Christmas, and in Cork in Ireland it remains part of traditional Christmas fare. It was once a favourite for hunt breakfasts and consequently is also known as huntsman's beef.

Potted beef is a rather different method of preserving meat, in that it is not necessarily salted, but is cooked and sealed under a layer of clarified butter or dripping, which keeps out airborne bacteria. The English writer Sir Hugh Plat (1552–1608) said that the meat would keep 'sound and sweet for three weeks or one whole month'. Cooks discovered that meat would keep better if it was chopped and mashed with butter or other fat before potting. The method is similar to that used for French rillettes, traditionally made from shredded pork. Salt and spices were usually included, ground pepper and mace being the most important, with ginger, cayenne, cloves and nutmeg as optional additions. In the eighteenth and nineteenth centuries England's potteries produced special containers for potted meats. Attractively decorated with designs that portrayed historic events or hunting scenes, they have become collectors' items.

Thrifty cooks may well have potted leftover cooked meat. Perhaps that was Hannah Glasse's intention in a recipe she published in 1747, 'To pot a cold tongue, beef or venison', in which the meat is chopped, pounded with butter and anchovies, pressed into pots and covered with clarified butter.

Potted beef today is something of a regional speciality. In Scotland, butchers sell it under the name potted hough (meaning hock or shin of beef).

DRIED BEEF

Drying meat in the sun or wind is an ancient preservation technique used by many cultures around the world. Removing moisture makes the meat less prone to bacterial infection; it also makes it lighter and therefore useful sustenance for travellers, as it is a good source of protein. Some of the most delectable dried meats are associated with mountainous areas, where the cold dry air allowed a long, slow cure. Nowadays, dried beef is usually served as a snack or as an appetizer, cut into very thin slices.

Bresaola, sometimes spelled brisaula, is spiced dried beef from northern Italy. The name may derive from the word *brasa*, referring to the braziers once used to smoke the meat, or from *brisa*, a dialect word referring to the salting process. The best-known is Bresaola della Valtellina, from an Alpine valley in northern Lombardy, on the border with Switzerland. The beef, from the hindquarters, is carefully trimmed of all fat and sinews, then dry-salted with a mixture of spices. After salting, the beef is stuffed into natural or artificial casings, dried and matured for up to three months. It is distinguished by its even, bright red colour (with a barely visible dark border), slightly aromatic smell and firm yet moist texture. It is generally served as a first course, sliced paper thin and drizzled with olive oil, lemon juice, a little black pepper and shavings of Parmesan cheese.

Bündnerfleisch, **Bindenfleisch** or **Viande des Grisons** is air-dried beef from the canton of Graubünden (Grisons) in the Swiss Alps. Traditionally the beef is treated with white wine, then cured with salt and herbs and hung up to dry for 10–15 weeks in the cool Alpine air. A similar product is made in the sub-Alpine Jura mountains of France: brési is thought to have been made since the sixteenth century and allegedly takes its name from its resemblance to brazilwood, an exotic hard red wood.

Cecina, from Spain, has a long history: it was known to Columella, a Roman soldier and farmer writing in the first century AD. Today, the finest is Cecina de León, from the region of Castilla y León in north-west Spain. This is made from the hindquarters of mature cattle; the meat is salted, usually smoked over oak, and then dried, the whole process taking at least seven months; some are cured for more than a year, resulting in a deeper flavour. The outside of the meat is brown and dry, while the inside is rich red with a light marbling of fat.

Jerky is a particularly well-travelled form of travellers' provision, originating in South America more than 500 years ago. The Inca Empire, centred on modern-day Peru, had an extensive road system. Inns along the way kept stocks of dried meat – probably made from domesticated llama, as it still is in parts of South America – which the Spanish conquistadors called *charqui*, adapted from the Quechua word *ch'arki*, 'dried meat'. It was first mentioned in English by the explorer Captain John Smith in his *Map of Virginia* (1612): he described a local meat prepared 'til it be as drie as their jerkin beefe in the West Indies, that they may keepe it a month or more, without putrifying'. 'Jerkin' was his interpretation of the Spanish name. Central and South America have many variations on *charqui*, or *carne seca* (dried meat), one of the best known being Brazil's *carne de sol* (meat of the sun).

The meat, usually beef, is trimmed of fat, cut into thin strips, dry salted or brined, then dried in the sun or smoked. Commercial jerky comes in a variety of flavours from different marinades, often sweet or semi-sweet. As it is light and nutritious, jerky has been chosen by astronauts to take on space flights.

Pastırma, **basturma** or **basturma** (and there are doubtless other spellings) is a highly seasoned, air-dried cured beef made in the Balkans, Turkey and the Middle East. The word is thought to come from the Romanian *pastra*, to preserve. After salting and partially drying, the meat is pressed and coated in spices such as cumin, paprika, fenugreek and garlic before the dry-curing is completed.

Biltong, best known as a South African snack with beer while watching rugby, evolved from European recipes brought by the seventeenth-century Dutch settlers. They desperately needed to preserve the meat of their livestock and hunted game animals, and soon developed the mildly spiced air-dried meat we know as biltong – from the Dutch *bil* ('buttock') and *tong* ('strip' or 'tongue').

The meat, typically beef, game animals or ostrich, is cut into strips about 2.5 cm/1 in thick, briefly marinated in vinegar, then rubbed with a mixture of salt, sugar and spices and hung up to dry. Drying time varies, but when cured the biltong is very dark and hard on the outside, yet still slightly moist on the inside. It is eaten as a snack, cut in thin slices.

Droëwors ('dry sausage') is similar to biltong, but made from minced beef.

Corned beef

Corned beef, or salt beef, gets its name from the 'corns' or grains of salt that are used to preserve it. The corned beef sold in cans is no more than a second cousin twice removed! The quality of the meat is paramount and a certain amount of fat essential: I like about 15 per cent fat. This recipe is based on a piece of brined beef, using the brine recipe on page 252 You need to brine it for at least 2 days, and I have left it for over 7 days.

SERVES 4–6

about 1.2 kg/2½ lb brisket,
  brined
2 carrots
1 onion, studded with
  8 cloves
base of a head of celery
1 head of garlic, cut in
  half horizontally
bay leaf, rosemary
  and thyme

Soak the brined beef in fresh cold water for about 2 hours. Put it in a deep pan and cover with cold water, slowly bring to the boil and skim off the grey scum. Add the rest of the ingredients and reduce to a gentle simmer, partially cover and cook for 3 hours or until tender.

Slice and serve hot, with boiled potatoes and mustard. Or slice thinly and make a sandwich, on rye bread with pickles and/or mustard.

Potted beef

Potted beef, especially potted hough (shin), is a Scottish speciality, sold in most butchers. I like to use brisket, as its fat keeps the dish moist. The traditional recipe doesn't use a brine, but I think that brining firms up the meat a little, while the other ingredients in the brine add to the flavour.

The addition of prunes came after a cooking session with my friend David Naylor, a chef who has worked at the legendary Sharrow Bay country house hotel in the Lake District. He sometimes comes up with some extraordinary ideas, but this works really well, as the prunes provide a lovely sweet counterpoint to the meat. I serve this spooned from the pot with toast and salad and my favourite piccalilli, but any tangy salsa will go well.

SERVES 6, AS A FIRST COURSE

about 400 g/14 oz freshly cooked corned beef (see opposite), with its cooking liquid
salt and pepper
10 stoneless ready-to-eat dried prunes, ideally Agen prunes, roughly chopped

Leave the corned beef in its cooking liquid to cool slightly, then remove from the pan. Simmer steadily to reduce the cooking liquid by half and then leave to cool.

Chop the beef into small chunks, mixing fat and lean, and season with a little salt (take care, especially if you have brined it for a long time) and black pepper. Mix in the prunes and add a little of the cooled stock, just enough to moisten (about 4 tbsp) and then cram it into an earthenware crock pot or bowl, cover and place in the fridge. It is best left for at least 48 hours before eating and will keep happily for up to a week.

THE OFTEN OVERLOOKED

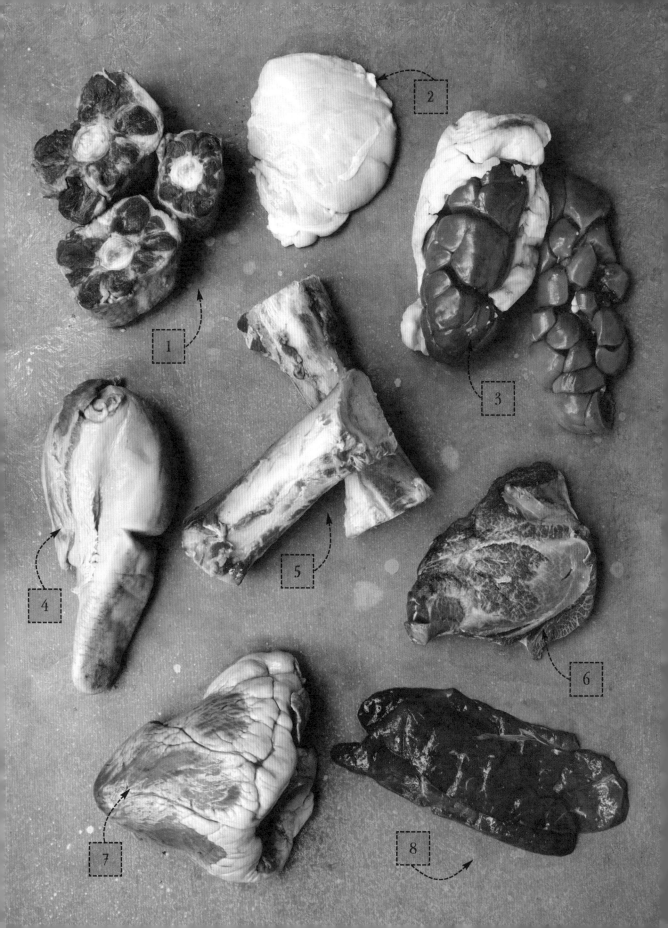

The best bits...

Offal, variety meats, organ meats, innards, entrails, bits and bobbles – however you put it, it doesn't sound great, but adventurous eaters know it can taste amazing, and the American term 'variety meats' does justice to the huge array of textures and flavours.

While sweetbreads have always been prized by gourmets, other parts, such as tripe and tail, have a more down-to-earth appeal. Until relatively recently, peasants sold their older animals and calves for meat and the butcher often gave them some of the offal as part payment. The important thing to remember is that offal must be used as fresh as possible, certainly within 24 hours of purchase.

1 **Oxtail** has a distinctive beefy flavour, but needs long, slow, moist cooking – in braises, stews or soups – until the meat falls off the bone.

2 **Sweetbreads** have a delicate flavour and melt-in-the-mouth texture. They are the thymus glands of the calf, which disappears as the animal matures. The round sweetbreads (sometimes called 'heart' sweetbreads) are considered superior to the elongated 'throat' sweetbreads. They are prepared by blanching and pressing before being braised, sautéed, fried or grilled.

3 **Veal kidneys** are multi-lobed (unlike lambs', pigs' and human kidneys). They have a rich flavour and firm yet tender texture; delicious sautéed or grilled. Ox kidneys have a stronger flavour and are used in stews, pies and the classic English steak and kidney pudding.

4 **Tongue** is sold either fresh or cured (brined or 'pickled'), from both calves and mature animals (sold as ox tongue). The meaty muscle is covered in a thick skin, which is easily peeled off after simmering. The tongue can then be cooked in various ways or eaten cold.

5 **Marrow bones** are prized for their delicate, wobbly, melt-in-the-mouth, fatty marrow. Split lengthways or across, they are poached or roasted and the marrow scooped out onto toast. The uncooked marrow is also used to enrich sauces such as bordelaise, a classic French accompaniment to steak.

6 **Cheek**, once trimmed of its fat, presents a solid piece of meat that responds well to long, gentle, moist cooking.

7 **Heart** is a dense, meaty muscle that can be sliced and cooked quickly over high heat, or tenderized by slow-roasting or braising.

8 **Liver** from a calf has a velvety texture and subtle flavour. It is at its best when cut into thin slices and quickly grilled or fried; larger pieces can be braised or quickly roasted. Ox liver is coarser in texture and flavour and may be soaked in milk before braising.

Offal from nose to tail

The cow is a valuable animal and all around the world people have risen to the challenge of making the most of every part. Old cookbooks include notes on cooking the marrow from the spine (ox pith, *amourettes* in French), the mesentery (an intestinal membrane, *fraise* in French) and the palate – for which there are ten recipes in Robert May's *The Accomplished Cook* (1660). Offal is a particular feature of the cuisine of Rome, where it is called the *quinto quarto* (fifth quarter): four 'quarters' of the carcass are hung and butchered, but it would be a shame to waste the rest!

Calf's head, known in France as *tête de veau*, remains a popular bistro dish; it is poached, sliced and served with a piquant gribiche or ravigote sauce to offset the rather bland and fatty meat. Boned calves' heads are often seen in French butchers' shops and supermarkets, looking like a sad grey mask. Clearly, some people are less squeamish than others. Mrs Beeton's *Book of Household Management* (1861) gives several recipes for calf's head – including instructions on how to carve it, with the tongue and brains served on a separate dish, as a main course to serve eight.

Calf's head was also used to make mock turtle soup. In the 1750s, turtles were imported into England from the West Indies and used to make a soup that quickly became famous; within a few years recipes for 'mock turtle' soup (made from calf's head rather than the expensive turtle) appeared. John Tenniel's illustrations for the first edition of Lewis Carroll's *Alice's Adventures in Wonderland* (1865) show the mournful Mock Turtle with a turtle's shell and the head, feet and tail of a calf. At Abraham Lincoln's inaugural luncheon in March 1861, the first course was mock turtle soup, followed by corned beef and cabbage, with blackberry pie for dessert. Still popular in 1912, Campbell's Mock Turtle soup was selling for 10 cents a can.

The head of a calf or ox can also be simmered until the meat is very tender, then set in jelly to make brawn (head cheese). In France the muzzle, or *museau*, is often prepared this way; it is served with vinaigrette, shallots and parsley.

Cheeks are so 'meaty' that they are barely identifiable as offal, and they can be used in place of stewing beef in slow-cooked recipes such as beef bourguignon. In November 1798 Jane Austen wrote to her sister Cassandra – Jane was left in charge while Cassandra was away and their mother was ill – 'I am very fond of experimental housekeeping, such as having an ox cheek now and then…with some little dumplings put into it'. Ox cheeks seemed to disappear over the culinary horizon during the twentieth century but have now been embraced by chefs rediscovering forgotten and inexpensive cuts.

Tongue: According to Alexandre Dumas, in the reign of Louis XII (1498–1515) tongues were so esteemed that the local squire had the right to the tongues of all slaughtered oxen. The French have a repertoire of classic dishes for *langue de boeuf* (ox tongue) and *langue de veau* (calf's tongue), usually served hot with a rich, slightly piquant sauce. Morocco, with many centuries of alliances with France, has its own tongue dishes with spicy sauces of cumin, chilli, paprika and a dash of vinegar. The combination of sweet and sour seems particularly well matched to tongue: Italy has its *lingua dolce-forte*, with chocolate, pine nuts, sugar and vinegar, and *lingua agro-dolce* with vinegar, sugar, sultanas and spices. Tongue is one of many elements of the classic northern Italian *bollito misto* (mixed boiled meats).

Cold tongue, cooked until tender and then pressed and sliced, speaks to generations of Brits as a picnic treat. In Kenneth Grahame's children's classic, *The Wind in the Willows* (1908), the Rat describes the contents of his picnic basket:

> *'There's a cold chicken inside it…*
> *coldtonguecoldhamcoldbeefpickledgherkinsalad…'!*

Smoked beef tongue is a speciality of north-east France. The town of Valenciennes is particularly associated with the luxurious *langue de boeuf Lucullus*, sliced smoked tongue with layers of foie gras. Smoked tongue is also popular in the Czech Republic, sometimes served with a plum sauce.

Brains: Calves' brains are very much a love-them-or-loathe-them delicacy, but aficionados can't get enough of their creamy texture. In a classic French dish, *cervelles au beurre noisette*, the brains are poached in a court bouillon; butter is heated until it begins to brown and then poured, sizzling hot, over the brains. One of Italy's favourite brain dishes is *cervella fritta* – the poached brains are coated in egg and breadcrumbs, fried until crisp and served with lemon. Brains with scrambled eggs emigrated from southern Germany to North America. *Tacos des sesos* (brain tacos) with salsa, onion and coriander (cilantro) are traditional in Mexico, while *Gulai otak* (brains in coconut curry) is popular in parts of Indonesia.

Feet: Elaborate jellies were central to medieval and Renaissance banquets: they came in all shapes and sizes and were brightly coloured, fancifully decorated, layered or gilded with gold or silver leaf. In preparation for a wedding feast, the anonymous author of *Le Ménagier de Paris* (a medieval manuscript dated c. 1393) advises his young wife to buy 'a hind leg of veal or veal feet, to make the liquid for the jelly.' Calves' feet (and the knuckle bone above) are rich in gelatine and relatively neutral in taste, so they were used for both savoury and sweet jellies. To extract the gelatine they must be boiled for several hours, and the resulting liquor is strained and clarified using egg whites. This laborious method of making jelly began to be superseded in the 1840s, with the advent of commercially produced gelatine. Calf's foot jelly, flavoured with lemon juice and wine, was recommended as a restorative for invalids until recent times.

Calves' feet and knuckles are just as indispensable to cooks today. Their natural gelatine gives body to veal stock, the fundamental ingredient of many important sauces.

The little feet are also eaten as a dish in their own right. In France they may be served with a poulette sauce (velouté enriched with egg yolks and flavoured with lemon juice and parsley). Morocco uses them in a tagine, and Anissa Helou, author of *Offal: The Fifth Quarter*, describes a Moroccan dish of calves' feet in a sweet and spicy honey sauce.

Cow heel, from animals over eight months old, is more strongly gelatinous than calf's foot and is the basis of many of the jellied dishes seen in French traiteurs (delicatessens). In twentieth-century Britain cow heel became particularly associated with Lancashire in north-west England; jellied cow heel was a popular dish during the summer 'wakes week' holidays.

Marrow, the pale pink, soft fatty substance found in the hollow leg bones, used to be given to children and invalids to 'build them up'. It was also used to enrich sweet puddings. A marrow pudding in John Nott's *The Cook's and Confectioner's Dictionary* (1723), made with breadcrumbs, eggs, marrow and sugar, is echoed by Mrs Beeton in her *Book of Household Management* (1861). Oliver Cromwell is said to have enjoyed marrow pudding at breakfast.

In the Georgian era marrow bones were baked – the ends sealed with a flour-and-water paste – then wrapped in a napkin and served with salt, pepper and wafer-thin toast. They were eaten with special long, silver marrow spoons. Queen Victoria was said to be fond of marrow on hot toast, sprinkled with parsley. In the twenty-first century roasted marrow bones are enjoying a renaissance in trendy bistros around the world.

Sweetbreads are much loved by gourmets and may be named for their rich, creamy delicacy, combined with the Old English word *braed*, meaning flesh. In France they are called *ris de veau* – of equally mysterious etymology.

Associated in classic French cuisine with luxurious garnishes and rich sauces, they have always been in demand at the best tables. Eliza Acton was tapping into the contemporary vogue for all things Indian when she gave a recipe for curried sweetbreads in *Modern Cookery for Private Families* (1845).

It was reported that in June 2010 British chef Heston Blumenthal cooked a private dinner for Queen Elizabeth II at Windsor Castle, at which he served a dish of sweetbreads, brains and testicles. Buckingham Palace declined to comment.

Heart, the muscle that never rests, can be tough, and many recipes call for it to be marinated to tenderize it; it can then be cubed or thinly sliced and cooked over high heat. In Peru, *anticuchos* are spicy marinated cubes of beef heart, cooked quickly on a barbecue.

Heart can also be tenderized by long, slow, moist cooking, and is sometimes stuffed. Typical country dishes from across Europe use heart in casseroles and braised dishes. Dorothy Hartley's *Food in England* (1954) tells how poor families in the north of England sometimes enjoyed a Christmas dinner of Mock Goose: an ox or bullock heart was simmered until very tender, then stuffed with sage and onions, covered with bacon rashers and roasted in the oven and served with roast potatoes and apple sauce.

Lungs, also known as lights, are not sold for human consumption in some countries, but remain popular in parts of southern Germany and Austria: the Austrian farmhouse dish of *Beuschel* combines lungs and heart. Neighbouring Hungary also uses heart and lungs in a variation of *pörkölt*, a stew with onions, paprika and peppers. The *lungen* stew of eastern European Jewish tradition may include cubed beef instead of heart. *Chanfainita*, the lung and potato stew of Peru, is becoming known further afield.

Blood: The Masai herdsmen of Kenya and Tanzania drink the blood of their cattle, without killing them, by cutting into a vein, taking some blood and then sealing the wound. It may sound ghoulish but mankind has long used blood as a source of energy. Ian Mortimer, in *The Time Traveller's Guide to Medieval England* (2008), tells how, in the fourteenth century, men would slice into their cattle's legs to obtain a little blood, which they mixed with oats and herbs – a rich source of protein. Cattle drovers in eighteenth-century Scotland did the same thing, to sustain them on their journey. An illustration in a French magazine in 1890 shows elegant ladies visiting the abattoir of La Villette in north-east Paris to drink a strengthening glass of ox blood.

Tripe is the English term for the four stomach compartments of the cow: the rumen (blanket/flat/smooth/thick-seam tripe), the reticulum (honeycomb/pocket tripe), the omasum (book/bible/leaf tripe) and the abomasum (reed tripe). In the UK and the US the most commonly seen tripe is honeycomb, sold ready prepared and pre-cooked ('blanched' or 'dressed'). **Rennet**, extracted from the stomachs of unweaned calves, is widely used in traditional cheesemaking,

Despite the fact that 'a load of tripe' is considered worthless, recipes for tripe can be found throughout Europe, Asia, Africa and the Americas – anywhere cows are eaten. Before tripe can be eaten, it needs to be repeatedly soaked and scrubbed clean, and then boiled for at least two or three hours. As with many foods, it's a bit of a mystery how man first decided tripe was good to eat.

Tripe has fallen from favour in many parts of Britain in recent decades. A similar trend was reported in France, but as times got tougher financially during the late 2000s the trend in France began to reverse. Older generations in the north of England have fond memories of tripe, but times have changed. Only a few dedicated tripe shops remain, whereas in 1908 there were over 200 tripe shops in Manchester alone and even in the early 1960s the UCP (United Cattle Products) had more than 100 tripe restaurants in the north-west.

Variety has always been the spice of tripe dishes. In Shakespeare's *The Taming of the Shrew*, a servant tempts Kate with 'a fat tripe, finely broil'd'. Hannah Glasse, in *The Art of Cookery made Plain and Easy* (1747), gives a recipe for pieces of tripe coated in batter and deep-fried. (In 1932 Ambrose Heath described a similar dish that he felt was certain to convert 'tripe-despisers'.) Victorian diners enjoyed stewed and curried tripe in popular supper rooms. 'Dressmaker tripe', a Norfolk recipe for tripe stuffed with breadcrumbs, onions, parsley and lemon, was popular in the 1930s. In the twentieth century, tripe and onions was a staple of the working-class diet, usually sprinkled with vinegar.

Onions also feature in a classic French regional tripe dish, *gras double à la lyonnaise* (*gras double* is a French term for tripe). Another speciality of the Lyonnais region is *tablier de sapeur* (sapper's apron), which got its name because the slices of tripe apparently resembled the leather aprons worn by engineers to protect their uniforms. But perhaps France's most famous tripe dish is *tripes à la mode de Caen*, originally from Normandy. The tripe is simmered with calf's foot, onions and carrots for many hours. In authentic versions Calvados is added before serving.

Italy has many regional variations on *trippa*, as does Spain for *callos*. In Mexico you'll find a hearty soup made of tripe, calves' feet and chillies, ironically named *menudo* (Spanish for small). It's often thought of as a hangover cure – if you can face this, you can face anything! The same principle applies to the traditional Bulgarian tripe soup, *skembe chorba*, which is often eaten 'the morning after'. Other countries of south-eastern Europe have their own versions of tripe soup, and it's also found in Turkey, as *iskembe corbasi*.

North America has, in general, spurned tripe for nearly a century, but Philadelphia pepper pot, a soup-stew made with tripe, pepper and lots of vegetables, is still well known, if not widely eaten. In the Caribbean and parts of South America *mondongo* sounds like a good word for the thick, spicy-hot tripe-based soup-stew.

Not surprisingly, in the parts of Asia where beef is eaten, nothing is wasted. Tripe is often an ingredient of a Chinese hotpot – but then so are a whole host of other ingredients, from pork belly to eel, squid, beans and greens. There are also many variations of tripe dim sum: the tripe may be poached in an aromatic broth and then stir-fried with ginger and spring onions or with garlic, chilli and coriander (cilantro).

Liver: Ox/beef liver has a strong flavour and is best suited to braising in a dish with other big flavours, such as onions, garlic and tomatoes. Calves' liver, on the other hand, is the finest of all the animal livers and must be cooked quickly so it retains its velvety texture. Simple flavourings are often the best.

Calves' liver pairs well with onions, in both the Venetian *fegato alla veneziana* and the French *foie de veau à la lyonnaise*. It's also good with sage, in a dish claimed by the Tuscans, *fegato alla salvia*. A slice of pancetta or bacon, either fried or grilled until crisp, is a great accompaniment to calves' liver.

Cream makes a rich sauce for a rich meat, but there's a touch of sharpness to both the Russian dish of liver with sour cream and the Austrian liver with cream and horseradish.

In Germany, Austria and Switzerland, light calves' liver dumplings (*Leberknödel*) are a traditional delicacy, made with breadcrumbs and poached.

Kidney: Ox/beef kidney needs long, slow cooking and is best in stews, steak and kidney pies and puddings. In *Les Soupers de la Cour* (1755), French master chef Menon includes a recipe for *Rognon de boeuf à la mode*, in which thin slices of ox kidney are layered in a casserole with bacon, interspersed with chopped spring onions (scallions), shallots, garlic and parsley and cooked in a low oven for 3 hours. In 1861 Mrs Beeton advises cutting a beef kidney into neat slices, soaking in water for 2 hours, drying them well and frying them in clarified butter. They are served with well-seasoned gravy, a dash of lemon juice and a pinch of sugar.

Veal kidneys, tender and rich, are a gourmet treat. Classic French dishes with origins dating back around 200 years that are still served today include veal kidney braised in port wine and sautéed kidney with a cream and mustard sauce.

Suet, the hard fat around the kidneys and loins, is used to make many of Britain's most-loved puddings, both sweet (such as roly poly) and savoury (steak and kidney), as well as dumplings and mincemeat for Christmas mince pies. Suet is quite different from beef **dripping**, which is the collected fat and juices from the roasting pan when cooking roast beef – used when making Yorkshire pudding and toad in the hole. A purified version of beef dripping is used to make excellent chips (French fries).

Udder appears to have been highly prized in the past. In Renaissance Rome, Bartolomeo Scappi, chef to cardinals and popes, gives several ways to cook a cow's udder in his *Opera* (1570). John Nott, writing in England in 1723, includes udder in a mighty stew with ox-palates and veal sweetbreads. Udder seems to be a vanishing delicacy, although there are occasional sightings in the markets of Florence (as *poppa*), in southern Germany (as *Euter* – for example, at the Weisses Bräuhaus tavern in Munich), and (as elder) in a few places in Lancashire and Yorkshire in northern England.

Testicles: Most bull calves are castrated, which makes them fatter and less aggressive – so there are always a couple of spare parts. What were once a cowboy's perks are now at the centre of the annual 'Rocky Mountain oyster fry' in Virginia City, Nevada. The 'oysters' are also known as prairie oysters, 'swinging beef' and, in Spanish-speaking ranches of Central and South America, as '*huevos del toro*' (bull's eggs) or *criadillas*. These days they are usually served sliced, floured and sautéed. In a recipe dating back to 1570, Bartolomeo Scappi, the personal cook to Pope Pius IV, includes them, sliced and sprinkled with salt, pepper, nutmeg and cinnamon, in a Pie of Bulls' Testicles.

Tail: Oxtails and calves' tails need long, slow cooking to tenderize the meat, but that problem was solved with the prehistoric invention of pottery and bronze cooking pots in which meat could be boiled or braised. Tails are also reluctant to give up their meat and do not make for elegant dining. Not an issue for the poor and hungry: throughout Europe, South America and the Caribbean there are many recipes for stews, daubes and braises made with oxtail (*queue de boeuf* in French, *coda di manzo* in Italian). If sucking the meat off the bones at table is not a preferred option, the cook can pick off the meat in the kitchen and use it in a chunky, vegetable-packed oxtail soup or a sparkling clear consommé. In *Modern Cookery for Private Families* (1845), Eliza Acton gives a recipe for Broiled Oxtail, in which the oxtail is first stewed until very tender, then drained, seasoned with salt and cayenne, dipped in butter and fine breadcrumbs and grilled until browned: it sounds very much like a modern recipe.

Braised beef cheeks with orange gremolata

Also known as ox cheeks, these are well worth seeking out for their rich, meaty flavour and tender, gelatinous texture. Each cheek usually weighs between 350 g/ 12 oz and 500 g/1 lb 2 oz, so you will need to buy two or three beef cheeks for this recipe. Some recipes suggest a marinade, but I don't think this is necessary with the long, slow cooking. If you like, replace half the stock with red wine.

SERVES 4

salt and pepper
about 1 kg/2¼ lb beef
  cheeks, trimmed
1–2 tbsp olive oil
1 tbsp butter
6 shallots, peeled
3 carrots, sliced thickly
  at an angle
500 ml/18 fl oz/2 cups beef
  stock
1 bay leaf
2–3 sprigs of thyme

ORANGE GREMOLATA
2 tbsp chopped fresh
  parsley
1 garlic clove, finely
  chopped
grated zest of 1 orange

Preheat the oven to 150°C/300°F/gas 2. Season the beef cheeks. Heat the olive oil in a hot ovenproof casserole and brown the cheeks all over. Remove from the pan and set aside. Add the butter and brown the shallots and carrots. Reduce the heat and return the meat to the pan, pour in the stock and bring to a simmer.

Add the herbs and cover with a cartouche – a disc of greaseproof paper cut to fit snugly in the pan, which really keeps the moisture in slow-cooked dishes. Cover with a lid and braise in the oven for 3½–4 hours. Check the liquid doesn't reduce too much and top up if necessary. When cooked, the meat should be tender enough to cut with a spoon. Remove from the heat and leave the meat to rest in the liquid for at least 30 minutes – or overnight.

To make the gremolata, mix together the parsley, garlic and orange zest.

Using a slotted spoon, lift out the meat and vegetables. Strain the liquid into another pan and simmer to reduce a little. Taste and check the seasoning. Return the meat and vegetables to the sauce to reheat. Slice the beef cheeks and serve with the shallots, carrots and a little of the sauce. Sprinkle a spoonful of gremolata over the cheeks before serving.

Tip

Geoffrey Smeddle, chef and owner of the Peat Inn near St Andrews in Scotland, allows the cheeks to cool completely and then rolls them tightly in clingfilm and leaves them in the fridge to firm up. This gives them a neat, even shape for slicing.

Ox tongue

Memories of pressed ox tongue from a can seem to dwell in my mind – this must be from school days, since I don't remember having it at home. Now I have revisited it – it's like a delicious new discovery! The salting process seems to help with tenderness as well as flavour. An ox tongue weighs about 1–2 kg/2¼–4½ lb and will serve 10–12 people, but don't be daunted – you can use the cooked tongue in any of the following recipes, and it makes wonderful sandwiches.

SERVES 10–12

brine (see page 252)
1 fresh ox tongue
celery trimmings
2 onions, peeled
2 leeks, trimmed
1 carrot, peeled
2 tsp black peppercorns
1 head of garlic, cut in
 half horizontally
1 cinnamon stick
2 bay leaves
a sprig of thyme
a sprig of rosemary

First make the brine and leave until cold. Rinse the ox tongue, then place in the brine and leave in a cool place for about 5–7 days.

Rinse the tongue and place in a large, deep pan with all the remaining ingredients, cover with fresh cold water and slowly bring to the boil. Skim off the grey scum. Reduce to a gentle simmer, partially cover and cook for 3–4 hours, or until tender when pierced with a skewer. Alternatively, it can be cooked overnight in a cool oven, 120°C/250°F/gas ½.

Leave in the liquid until cool enough to handle. Lift out the tongue and remove the skin; trim away any bone and gristle from around the root. Reserve the cooking liquid for use in other recipes if desired. You can serve the tongue hot, cut into 5 mm/¼ in thick slices, or press it and serve it cold.

To press, find a soufflé dish or cake tin into which the tongue will fit snugly. Curl the tongue into the dish with the tip in the centre. Cover and weight it down, and leave overnight in a cool place.

Piquant sauce

Here's a luxurious sauce to go with the tongue, served hot.

55 g/2 oz/4 tbsp butter
2 tsp brown sugar
2 tbsp plain (all-purpose)
  flour, sifted
450 ml/16 fl oz/scant
  2 cups cooking liquid
  (see opposite)
1 bay leaf
4 tbsp double (heavy)
  cream
150 ml/5 fl oz/⅔ cup dry
  (Sercial or Verdelho)
  Madeira
salt and pepper
2 tsp lemon juice
¼ tsp cayenne

Melt the butter in a saucepan, sprinkle in the sugar and allow to caramelize lightly. Add the flour and cook until light brown, stirring continuously. Now stir in the cooking liquid, a little at a time, then add the bay leaf and simmer gently for 20 minutes.

Take the pan from the heat, remove the bay leaf and stir in the cream and Madeira. Season well, adding the lemon juice and cayenne to taste.

Carve the tongue into thin slices, arrange on a warm plate and pour over some of the sauce. Serve any remaining sauce separately.

Tongue, beetroot & celeriac salad

A delightful first course to use up the last of the tongue, if there is any!

SERVES 4

about 300 g/11 oz cooked
   tongue
2 tsp Dijon mustard
2 tbsp olive oil
1 tbsp white wine vinegar
squeeze of lemon juice
1 tbsp chopped fresh
   parsley
salt and pepper
2 medium beetroots,
   either roasted or lightly
   boiled, peeled
4–5 gherkins
200 g/7 oz piece
   of celeriac, peeled

Slice the tongue thinly and place on 4 plates.

Whisk together the mustard, oil and vinegar, add the lemon juice
and parsley and season to taste.

Slice the beetroots, gherkins and celeriac into thickish matchsticks
and mix with the dressing. Strew over the meat.

Tip

The gherkins and beetroot can be
sliced in advance, but the celeriac
needs to go straight into the
dressing or else it will discolour.

Tongue with caper sauce

It sounds rather Victorian, and perhaps Charles Dickens enjoyed something
similar, but this piquant, moreish sauce is well worth a try.

SERVES 4

12 slices of cooked tongue
1 egg, beaten
about 85g/3 oz/2 cups
   fresh breadcrumbs
oil and butter for shallow-
   frying

CAPER SAUCE
25 g/1 oz/2 tbsp butter
1 onion, finely chopped
25 g/1 oz/3 tbsp plain
   (all-purpose) flour
1 tbsp white wine vinegar
500 ml/18 fl oz/2 cups
   cooking liquid (see page
   178), heated
2 tbsp chopped fresh
   parsley
2 tbsp capers, rinsed and
   patted dry
1 tbsp double (heavy)
   cream

To make the sauce, melt the butter in a saucepan over a medium-low heat,
add the onion and gently soften in the butter. Stir in the flour and cook for
a minute or two. Add the vinegar and then gradually stir in the hot
cooking liquid. When the sauce is smooth, simmer for 4 minutes to thicken
slightly. Add the parsley and capers and taste for seasoning: it probably
won't need salt. Finally, stir in the cream.

Meanwhile, dip the tongue slices in beaten egg, then in breadcrumbs to
coat. Fry over a medium heat until brown on both sides. Serve hot, with
the caper sauce. Mashed potatoes go well with this.

Braised calf's tongue with creamed leeks

Calf's tongue can be brined like the ox tongue (see page 178), but as it's younger I don't feel it is necessary. You can treat it the same way as the ox tongue, but I think a more delicate sauce is appropriate. The tender texture of the tongue combined with the creamy leeks is just knockout!

SERVES 4

1 calf's tongue
1 celery stalk, roughly chopped
1 small onion, studded with 5 cloves
1 head of garlic
6 peppercorns
4 leeks, thinly sliced
125 ml/4 fl oz/½ cup double (heavy) cream
½ tsp mustard
salt and pepper
1–2 tbsp chopped fresh parsley

Place the tongue in a deep pan with the celery, onion, garlic and peppercorns and cover with cold water. Slowly bring to the boil and skim off the grey scum. Reduce to a gentle simmer, partially cover and cook for 2–3 hours, or until tender when pierced with a skewer. Leave the tongue to cool in the stock. When cool enough to handle, peel off the skin: this is easy once you get a sharp knife under the first piece, then you can use your fingers. Strain the stock and set aside.

Preheat the oven to 180°C/350°F/gas 4. Slice the tongue into 8 pieces. Spread the sliced leeks in an ovenproof dish and place the tongue slices evenly on top. Pour in 200 ml/7 fl oz of the reserved stock and cook in the oven, basting occasionally, for about 30 minutes. When the meat is hot and the leeks softened, lift them out and keep warm, covered to prevent them from drying out.

Strain the juices into a saucepan, add another 100 ml/3½ fl oz/scant ½ cup stock and reduce rapidly to about 5 tbsp liquid. Meanwhile, put the leeks in another saucepan, add the cream and mustard and simmer until lightly thickened. Season to taste.

Place the leeks on 4 warmed plates, top with 2 slices of tongue and drizzle the reduced juices around the outside. Sprinkle with parsley. Serve with chunks of fresh bread to mop up the juices.

Oxtail stew

A true classic and one that has come full circle: once the food of the peasant, it now graces the menus of many innovative chefs, sometimes as a stew but also as soup or in ravioli. Your butcher will cut the oxtail into pieces for you. This recipe is fairly traditional, but I have added honey for extra depth of flavour. Like so many dishes of its kind, this stew is better served next day.

SERVES 6

25 g/1 oz/2 tbsp beef dripping
125 g/4¹/₂ oz unsmoked streaky bacon, diced
2 onions, chopped
3 carrots, diced
3 celery stalks, diced
2 oxtails (about 2 kg/4–4¹/₂ lb in total), cut into pieces
2 tbsp seasoned flour
2 garlic cloves, crushed
150 ml/5 fl oz/²/₃ cup red wine
2 tsp honey
2 tsp tomato purée
bay leaf, sprig of thyme, parsley stalks
salt and pepper
3 tbsp chopped fresh parsley

Preheat the oven to 160°C/325°F/gas 3. Heat the dripping in a large ovenproof pan and sauté the bacon for a few minutes, then add the onions, carrots and celery; cook until softened and then remove and set aside.

Roll the oxtail pieces in the seasoned flour and brown all over in the hot pan – you will need to do this in batches. Stir in the garlic and then the red wine, allowing it to bubble up before adding the honey, tomato purée, bay, thyme and parsley stalks. Add cold water to just cover the oxtail and bring to a simmer, then cover and cook in the oven for about 3 hours.

At this point you can either skim off as much fat as possible before continuing with the recipe, or set the pan aside and chill overnight. The fat will solidify and will be easy to lift off the next day.

Return the diced vegetables to the pan and cook for a further 1–1½ hours, until the meat is tender and falling off the bone.

Using a slotted spoon, lift out the pieces of oxtail and set aside. Strain the sauce into another large pan and remove the flavouring herbs, setting aside the diced vegetables. Bring the sauce to the boil and reduce to thicken slightly. Season to taste. Return the oxtail and vegetables to the sauce, stir in the chopped parsley and serve hot, with mashed potatoes.

Tip

Instead of fresh chestnuts, you could use vacuum-packed cooked chestnuts – add them about 30 minutes before the end of the cooking time.

Oxtail & stout soup

For this recipe you can use just the narrow end of the oxtail. With the addition of chestnuts and beer, this rich broth is a meal in itself.

SERVES 6

450 g/1 lb chestnuts
1 oxtail or two of the
  narrow ends (about
  1–1.5 kg/2–3½ lb in
  total), cut into pieces
2 tbsp seasoned flour
2 tbsp olive oil
2 onions, chopped
2 carrots, chopped
2 tsp sea salt
freshly ground black
  pepper
500 ml/18 fl oz/2 cups
  dark beer or stout
1 litre/1¾ pints/4 cups
  water

Using a small sharp knife, make a slit in each chestnut and then put them under a hot grill for 5–10 minutes, turning occasionally; it should now be easy to cut off the hard shells and wafery inner skins; set aside.

Roll the oxtail pieces in the seasoned flour, shaking off any excess. Heat the oil in a large pan over a medium-high heat and brown the oxtail all over; remove and set aside. Turn down the heat, add the onions and carrots and soften for 5–10 minutes, then add the chestnuts, return the oxtail and season with the salt and pepper. Add the beer and top up with the water, bring to the boil and simmer for about 2–2½ hours, or until the meat is tender.

Using a slotted spoon, lift out the bones and take off as much meat you can; set aside. Skim off as much fat as possible, then blend the vegetables and liquid in a food processor. Return to the pan, add the meat and reheat if necessary. Check for seasoning and serve with good crusty bread.

Veal heart in red wine

Veal heart is very versatile and can be cooked in various ways. The basic preparation is much the same as for any meat: trim off sinew and excess fat and wipe or rinse off any blood – ask your butcher to do this for you, if you prefer.

Try slicing it thinly – 5 mm/¼ in thick – and cooking it like a skirt steak – quickly, over a high heat – and leave it to rest for a few minutes before serving with a crisp salad. You can also stuff it with the stuffing for the breast of veal (see pages 243–244) and slow cook it on a bed of vegetables with a little white wine.

I like to cook it in red wine, either with mushrooms or with fennel, which gives a delicious fresh flavour. Instead of using rosemary or sage, you could stir in a tablespoon of chopped fresh tarragon 10–15 minutes before serving. Roast Jerusalem artichokes are an excellent vegetable accompaniment.

SERVES 4

1 calf's heart, trimmed
  and cut into 2 cm/³/₄ in
  chunks
1–2 tbsp seasoned flour
1 tbsp olive oil
25 g/1 oz/2 tbsp butter
200 g/7 oz button
  mushrooms
1 onion, chopped
2 tsp tomato purée
125 ml/4 fl oz/¹/₂ cup
  red wine
200 ml/7 fl oz/generous
  ³/₄ cup stock
1 tsp chopped fresh
  rosemary or sage
salt and pepper

Preheat the oven to 150°C/300°F/gas 2.

Toss the heart in seasoned flour and shake off any excess. Heat a heavy-bottomed pan, add the oil and butter; when the butter foams, add the heart and brown all over. Place in a casserole dish.

Add the mushrooms to the pan and colour quickly, then add to the casserole. Add the onion to the pan and cook until softened, then stir in the tomato purée and red wine, allow to bubble up and then add the stock, bring to the boil and pour over the meat and mushrooms. Stir in the rosemary or sage, cover and cook in the oven for 2–3 hours, until tender. Taste for seasoning before serving.

Variation

Veal heart with fennel

Replace the mushrooms with
2 quartered fennel bulbs.

Calves' brains

These always bring back memories of my days in the Savoy kitchen in London. We used to cook calves' heads and serve them with a vinaigrette; I remember always having trouble preparing them, as I couldn't face the calves' long eyelashes! So I'm not including a recipe for calf's head: if you want to try it, you'll have to go to France, where *tête de veau* is still a popular dish.

Calves' brains, however, posed no such problem, and I think they are quite delicious, with their velvety, creamy texture. They do need some advance preparation.

PREPARING BRAINS

To remove the blood, soak the brains in cold water for about 2 hours, changing the water from time to time. I think it's a matter of choice whether you trim them before or after poaching, but they are very wobbly before cooking and can be hard to sort! So, first make a light court bouillon: in a pan that will hold the brains comfortably, put some onion slices, a few peppercorns, a bay leaf, parsley stalks or other herbs, 1 tbsp white wine vinegar and about 1.5 litres/2½ pints/6 cups cold water, and bring to the boil. Add the brains and poach at a gentle simmer for 20 minutes. Drain and leave to cool, then chill in the fridge. Using a pair of scissors and your fingers, peel off the membrane.

Calves' brains with lemon & capers

One of the simplest and best ways to cook brains; they should have a light crust on the outside and be meltingly creamy on the inside.

SERVES 4

2 calves' brains, prepared and cut into 2 cm/³/4 in thick slices

2 tbsp seasoned flour

2 tbsp olive oil

2 tsp butter

2 tsp capers, rinsed

juice of 1 lemon, plus lemon wedges to serve

2 tbsp chopped fresh parsley

Toss the sliced brains lightly in the seasoned flour and shake off any excess. Heat a large frying pan (skillet) over a medium-high heat and add the olive oil. When the oil is hot, add half the butter and as it fizzles up add the brains. Brown lightly for 6–8 minutes, turning once. Drain on kitchen paper and keep warm.

Add the capers and toss in the pan juices, add the remaining 1 teaspoon butter, the lemon juice and parsley, stir briefly and pour over the brains. Serve immediately, with lemon wedges.

Calves' liver

This is one of my favourite treats; quick and simple to cook, and best with the simplest of ingredients.

PREPARING LIVER

Allow about 125 g/4½ oz per person, which is two good slices. Ask your butcher to trim away any tubes (veins): these turn rubbery when cooked. The liver should not be cut too thinly –about 1–1.5 cm/½–¾ in – because it needs to cook quickly but still be meltingly tender on the inside.

Coat the liver slices in seasoned flour and shake off any excess. Heat a large frying pan (skillet) over a high heat, add 1–2 tbsp butter and when it is just foaming but not quite brown add the liver. Cook for about 2 minutes on each side until golden brown. Remove to a warm plate and rest for a few minutes before serving.

With sage
After you've removed the liver, throw some roughly chopped sage leaves into the pan, add a squeeze of lemon juice, stir briefly and then pour over the liver.

With onions
Before you cook the liver, prepare some caramelized onions: this can be done in advance. Heat 1 tbsp oil in a deep frying pan (skillet), add 1 tbsp butter and then add some thinly sliced onions (allow 1 per person and 1 extra) and cook for about 20–30 minutes over a medium-low heat: you want the onions to be soft and browned, but not burnt. While the liver is resting, add the onions to the pan and heat through.

With vinegar
After you've removed the liver, add a good splash of vinegar: balsamic, sherry, red or white wine vinegar.

Vinegar is also good added to caramelized onions as a counterpoint to their sweetness.

With bacon
Cook slices of unsmoked streaky bacon quickly in the pan after you've removed the liver. Put the bacon on top of the liver, then add a little more butter to the bacon juices, allow to bubble up and then pour over the liver and bacon.

Kidneys

To highlight the sublime tenderness of veal kidneys, I love them simply grilled
and topped with a flavoured butter (see page 56). If you can get them still in their
casing of fat, trim the layer of fat to about 1 cm/½ in all over, then roast them
whole at 190°C/375°F/gas 5 for about 1 hour; as the fat melts, it bastes the
kidney, keeping it tender and juicy.

Ox kidneys have a strong flavour and are best used in a steak and kidney pie
or pudding (see page 137).

PREPARING KIDNEYS

If you buy kidneys in their fat, cut into the fat with a small sharp knife and gently pull it away.
The surface membrane can be cut off in the same way. Cut the kidneys lengthwise and then snip
out the core of fat, using scissors. Your butcher may do some or all of this for you.

Kidneys with creamed endive

Here is a lovely idea from a former colleague at the Savoy, chef Aidan McCormack. He went on to become head chef at Middlethorpe Hall in Yorkshire. His combination of chicory (Belgian endive) with kidneys is excellent.

SERVES 4

2 lemons
175 g/6 oz/³/₄ cup butter
1 shallot, finely chopped
1 tbsp clear honey
300 ml/10 fl oz/1¹/₄ cups
  veal stock
salt and pepper
450 g/1 lb chicory (Belgian
  endive), finely sliced
4 tbsp double (heavy)
  cream
2 tbsp vegetable oil
2 veal kidneys, fat and core
  removed, then cut into
  1 cm/¹/₂ in slices

Cut the peel from the lemons into thin strips – avoid taking too much of the white pith – and blanch in boiling water for 1 minute. Refresh in cold water. Squeeze the lemon juice and set aside.

Heat 25 g/1 oz/2 tbsp of the butter in a small pan and cook the shallot until softened but not browned. Add the honey and caramelize lightly, whisk in the lemon juice and simmer for a minute, then add the veal stock and reduce until syrupy. Whisk in 100 g/3½ oz/6 tbsp butter, season and strain into a clean pan. Add the blanched lemon strips.

Meanwhile, heat 25 g/1 oz/2 tbsp of the butter in a pan and cook the chicory over a low heat for 5 minutes. Add the cream, boil until slightly thickened, season to taste and set aside.

Heat a deep frying pan (skillet), add the oil and then add the remaining butter; when the butter fizzles add the kidneys, season and cook quickly, stirring to turn them in the hot fat – this will take less than 2 minutes. Leave to rest in a warm place for a few minutes before serving.

Divide the chicory between 4 warmed plates, add the kidneys and pour over the sauce. Serve immediately, with new potatoes.

Kidneys with mustard & whisky

Some chopped parsley is good in this dish, though not essential.

SERVES 4

1 tbsp wholegrain mustard
4 tbsp double (heavy) cream
1 tbsp olive oil
40 g/1½ oz/3 tbsp butter
2 veal kidneys, fat and core removed, then sliced into small chunks
1 tbsp whisky
salt and pepper
1 tbsp chopped fresh parsley (optional)

Mix the mustard with the cream.

Heat the oil in a deep frying pan (skillet) and when hot add the butter, then immediately add the kidneys, turning them frequently until they are evenly cooked and lightly browned.

After about 4 minutes, reduce the heat and add the whisky: take care if cooking over a flame because it might ignite for a second! Stir in the cream and mustard mixture and season to taste. Add the parsley, if using. Stir to coat and heat through. Serve hot, with pilaf rice.

Variation

Kidneys with cream and mushrooms
Mix the mustard with 100 ml/3½ fl oz/6 tbsp double (heavy) cream. After the kidneys are lightly browned, remove from the pan, using a slotted spoon, and keep warm. Add 140 g/5 oz sliced mushrooms and cook over a high heat until softened. Add the cream and mustard mixture and bring just to the boil, then return the kidneys to the pan and heat through.

Kidneys with sage & balsamic vinegar

Sage and veal is a marriage made in heaven and this applies to the offal as well. Shallots and balsamic vinegar round out the flavours.

SERVES 4

2 veal kidneys, fat and core
  removed, then sliced into
  small chunks
salt and pepper
1 tbsp olive oil
4 tsp butter
3 shallots, finely chopped
12 sage leaves
1 tsp balsamic vinegar

Season the kidneys. Heat a deep frying pan (skillet), add the oil and then add half the butter; when the butter fizzles add the kidneys and cook quickly until they are sealed and lightly browned, but do not overcook. Remove them to a warm plate and keep warm.

Reduce the heat, add the shallots and stir until softened. Add the remaining butter and then the sage leaves and lastly the balsamic. Return the kidneys to the pan together with any juices and heat through. Serve hot, with steamed spinach and mashed potato.

Sweetbreads

Sweetbreads — *ris de veau* in French — appear on many fine restaurant menus. The basic preparation is a bit tricky, but well worth it. After they have been poached and pressed you can keep them, covered, in the fridge overnight.

PREPARING SWEETBREADS

First soak the sweetbreads to remove any blood: this ensures that they are pale-coloured and delicately flavoured. Then they are poached (see page 198) to firm up the texture. It's important to remove the tough membrane and fat so that the finished dish is silky-smooth.

Basic sweetbreads

It can be a little daunting to cook sweetbreads. Here is a basic method for poaching and pressing them.

4 veal sweetbreads
  (about 900 g/2 lb in total)
1 carrot, sliced
1 small onion or shallot,
  sliced
1 small celery stalk, sliced
1 bay leaf
sprig of thyme
2 star anise
pinch of salt
1 tbsp white wine vinegar

Soak the sweetbreads in cold water for 1–2 hours, changing the water two or three times.

Make a light court bouillon: put the carrot, onion, celery, bay leaf, thyme, star anise, salt and vinegar into a pan that will hold the sweetbreads comfortably. Add about 1.5 litres/2½ pints/6 cups cold water, and bring to the boil. Add the sweetbreads and poach at a gentle simmer for about 15 minutes. Drain and refresh in cold water.

Pick off any bits of fat and remove the membrane from the sweetbreads, using your fingers. Don't remove the thinner membrane, or the sweetbreads will fall apart when you cook them.

Put them on a plate, cover with another plate and put a weight on top; leave for 1–2 hours.

Variation

Fried sweetbreads

Cut the pressed sweetbreads into 2 cm/¾ in thick slices. Lightly coat the sweetbreads in seasoned flour, then dip them in well-beaten egg to coat evenly, then finally dip them in fine fresh white breadcrumbs and fry in oil and butter until golden. Serve with Béarnaise sauce (see page 55).

Sweetbreads with Drambuie

My favourite way of cooking sweetbreads is in this creamy sauce.

SERVES 4

about 800 g/1³/₄ lb
  sweetbreads, prepared
25 g/1 oz/2 tbsp butter
200 g/7 oz small button
  mushrooms
200 ml/7 fl oz/generous
  ³/₄ cup veal stock
3 tbsp Drambuie
200 ml/7 fl oz/generous
  ³/₄ cup double (heavy)
  cream
salt and pepper
¹/₂ lemon

Cut the pressed sweetbreads into 2 cm/¾ in thick slices. Cook gently in the butter over a medium heat, turning occasionally, for about 5 minutes. Remove from the pan and keep warm.

Increase the heat, add the button mushrooms and cook for 4 minutes, then add the stock and reduce by half. Add the Drambuie and cream and simmer to reduce to a coating consistency. Season and add a squeeze of lemon juice to taste. Pour over the sweetbreads and serve immediately.

Tripe with Riesling

This dish originates in Alsace, France, using the local dry Riesling wine. You could substitute another lemony, fragrant dry wine, such as dry Muscat or Chenin Blanc – but don't use an oaky wine. This is a simple idea, which enhances the texture and flavour of the meat. You can order ready-prepared – cleaned and partially cooked – honeycomb tripe from your butcher.

SERVES 4

1 kg/2¼ lb prepared honeycomb tripe
1 large onion, finely sliced
1 tbsp butter
100 ml/3½ fl oz/scant ½ cup double (heavy) cream
1 tbsp tomato purée
125 ml/4 fl oz/½ cup dry Riesling wine
2 tbsp Dijon mustard
1 tbsp chopped fresh chives, plus extra for sprinkling
salt and pepper
lemon juice

Cut the tripe into 3 cm/1¼ in squares.

In a heavy-bottomed pan with a well-fitting lid, gently cook the onion in the butter over a low heat until softened. Add the tripe and stir in the cream and tomato purée. Cover and cook very gently for about 30–40 minutes until tender.

Add the wine, mustard and chives and bring to the boil. Season with salt and pepper to taste, add a squeeze of lemon juice, sprinkle with chives and serve hot, with new potatoes or pasta.

Tips

- If you like, add 55 g/2 oz chopped smoked bacon when softening the onions.

- Depending on the tripe you buy, it may take a longer or shorter time to cook: some tripe may be tender after 20 minutes, other tripe may take up to 1 hour. Test for tenderness with the point of a knife.

Roast marrow bones

The marrow from veal shins (shanks) has had its moments in history: eighteenth-century diners used special silver spoons to scoop out the rich marrow. It is currently enjoying a renaissance, partly, I am sure, thanks to Fergus Henderson's roast bone marrow and parsley salad, a signature dish at his London restaurant, St John.

1, 2 or 3 pieces of veal shin
  bone per person
toast, such as sourdough
plenty of finely chopped
  fresh parsley
sea salt

The number of bones you need will depend partly on their size and partly on what else you are serving, but be warned, the marrow is very rich.

It really doesn't matter whether the bones are sawn across into 6–8 cm/2½–3 in cylinders, or lengthwise, exposing the marrow.

Preheat the oven to 220°C/425°F/gas 7. Stand the cylinders upright or lay the long bones cut-side up in a roasting tin, and roast in the hot oven for 15–20 minutes. Serve the marrow bones hot from the oven; scoop out the marrow and spread it on toast; sprinkle with chopped parsley and sea salt.

VEAL

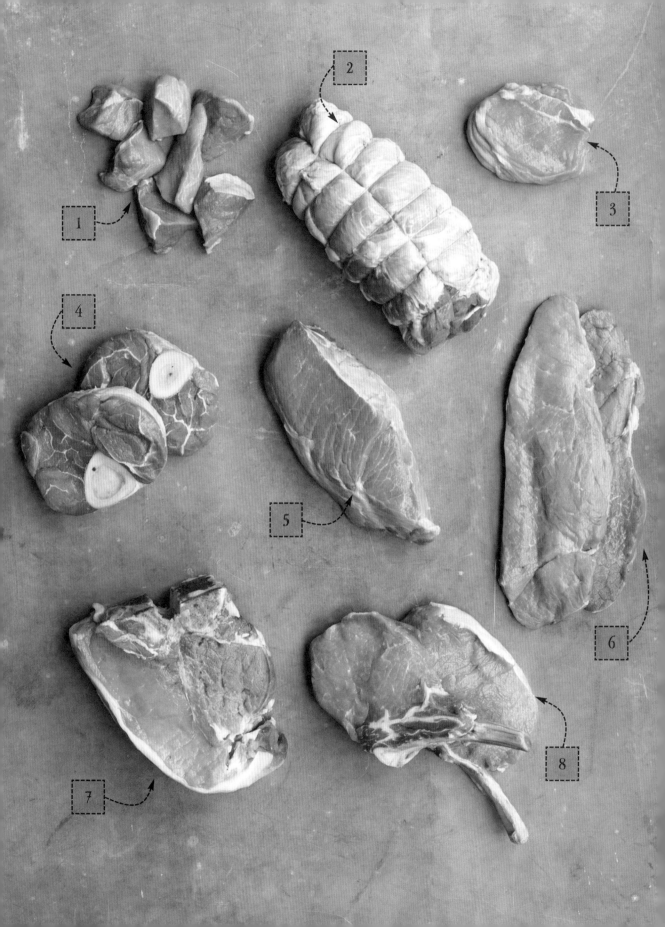

Veal cuts

In mainland Europe, veal remains popular at all levels of society, and has an important role in the national cuisines of Italy, France, Germany and Austria. Meanwhile, in Britain and North America veal consumption has fallen dramatically since the 1940s – partly due to the impact of anti-cruelty campaigns from the 1970s onwards. But as welfare issues are being addressed and rose or red veal (see page 216) becomes more readily available, we can now reintroduce veal to our culinary repertoire, whether in the form of tender escalopes, juicy veal chops, or an Italian-style pot-roast, meltingly tender after two or three hours in the oven.

As veal is so lean, it generally responds best to gentle heat and moist cooking methods, although tender cuts such as escalopes, cutlets and chops are most succulent when cooked quickly over high heat. For more about the different cuts of veal, see pages 32–33.

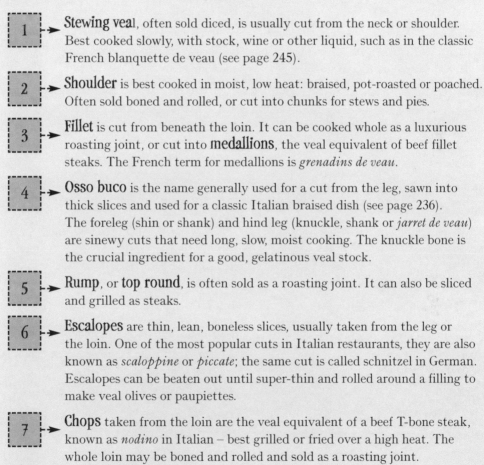

1 **Stewing veal**, often sold diced, is usually cut from the neck or shoulder. Best cooked slowly, with stock, wine or other liquid, such as in the classic French blanquette de veau (see page 245).

2 **Shoulder** is best cooked in moist, low heat: braised, pot-roasted or poached. Often sold boned and rolled, or cut into chunks for stews and pies.

3 **Fillet** is cut from beneath the loin. It can be cooked whole as a luxurious roasting joint, or cut into **medallions**, the veal equivalent of beef fillet steaks. The French term for medallions is *grenadins de veau*.

4 **Osso buco** is the name generally used for a cut from the leg, sawn into thick slices and used for a classic Italian braised dish (see page 236). The foreleg (shin or shank) and hind leg (knuckle, shank or *jarret de veau*) are sinewy cuts that need long, slow, moist cooking. The knuckle bone is the crucial ingredient for a good, gelatinous veal stock.

5 **Rump**, or **top round**, is often sold as a roasting joint. It can also be sliced and grilled as steaks.

6 **Escalopes** are thin, lean, boneless slices, usually taken from the leg or the loin. One of the most popular cuts in Italian restaurants, they are also known as *scaloppine* or *piccate*; the same cut is called schnitzel in German. Escalopes can be beaten out until super-thin and rolled around a filling to make veal olives or paupiettes.

7 **Chops** taken from the loin are the veal equivalent of a beef T-bone steak, known as *nodino* in Italian – best grilled or fried over a high heat. The whole loin may be boned and rolled and sold as a roasting joint.

8 **Cutlets** from the best end of neck or centre ribs can be quickly fried, grilled or barbecued over a high heat. A rib roasting joint comprises two or more ribs.

A rich culinary tradition

When we read of veal in centuries-old cookbooks, we cannot know whether the veal was from a very young animal, raised specifically for its pale flesh, or from an older calf that had grazed alongside its mother for several months, whose meat would be deep pink and subtly beefy, like today's rose or red veal. But as so many early sources refer to veal, it seems certain that it was appreciated as a delicate meat quite distinct from beef.

The Romans' taste for young calves, baby lamb and suckling pig was so great that the Emperor Alexander Severus (AD 222–235) issued a decree forbidding their slaughter, since the breeding stock was being depleted. The only surviving recipe book from Roman times, *Apicius*, includes recipes for veal (and other meats) with sauces of honey, vinegar, *liquamen* (a salty fish sauce), herbs and spices such as cumin, oregano and fennel seed. The complexity of these sauces was echoed in the cooking of early medieval Europe.

'The Butcher's: Veal' is one of many illustrations in *Tacuinum Sanitatis Codex Vindobonensis,* a fourteenth-century handbook on health and wellbeing.

An Anglo-Norman manuscript from the early fourteenth century describes 'Haucegeme', a veal stew made from minced and diced veal, almond milk, galingale, cinnamon and sugar, which was coloured red. Taillevent (c.1312–1395), who began as a kitchen boy turning the roasting spits and became master chef to the French royal household, compiled one of the first published cookery books. His recipe for 'Civé de Veel' includes onions and as many spices as a modern Indian curry. The calf was prized not only for its meat (especially the sweetbreads and other organs) but also for the gelatine obtained from its feet: every feast needed eye-catching jellies, savoury and sweet, in bright colours and elaborate shapes.

The European Renaissance was led by Italy, rediscovering the culture of classical Rome. Ideas about science and art – including the art and science of cooking – were exchanged between the courts of dukes, princes and kings throughout Europe. *De honesta voluptate et valetudine* ('On honest pleasure and health') was an influential book by the Italian writer Platina, with recipes provided by the master cook Martino. Published in 1474, it included some recipes that would not be out of place today, such as veal olives rolled around parsley and marjoram and veal 'kebabs' – skewered pieces of veal sprinkled with salt and ground fennel and cooked over a fire.

From the late thirteenth century, the Italian nobility had shown a clear preference for light meats such as poultry (chicken, young pigeon, partridge) and veal. At the beginning of the fifteenth century, Italian physician Lorenzo Sassoli advised one of his distinguished patients 'to put veal into your body in any way you can, since with all its good properties, you will find no healthier form of food.' Veal was considered to be lighter, more digestible than the heavier beef preferred in northern Europe.

Some writers attributed Italy's preference for veal to its Mediterranean climate. The Italian scholar Giacomo Castelvetro, in exile in England in 1614, wrote a treatise encouraging the English to eat more fruit and vegetables. He pointed out that:

> *...you never have to endure, as we do in Italy, the loss of appetite caused by the intense summer heat. We like to revive our jaded palates with sharp things, and so we put sour gooseberries in sauces for chicken, squabs and boiled veal.*

Fifty years later, Englishman Robert May's *The Accomplisht Cook* (1660) includes a recipe for 'Minced pies in the Italian fashion', made with veal, gooseberries, currants and sugar.

It is sometimes said that Catherine de Medici, daughter of the ruling Florentine family, brought Renaissance cooking to France when she arrived with her entourage in 1533, to marry the future King Henry II of France. That may be oversimplifying the case, but it is clear that the vogue in France for all things Italian took off, and the Italian cooks' attention to detail and harmony had far-reaching effects throughout Europe. By about 1600 France had taken its place as a major centre of European culture, with a taste for luxury.

Various systems for rearing calves for veal are documented throughout history. The practice of killing them at just a few days old has regularly been condemned as barbaric. At the other extreme, in sixteenth-century Italy calves were sometimes fed entirely on milk for six months or up to a year. When the aristocratic taste for veal arrived in France, calves were allegedly fed on milk, egg yolks and biscuits.

Although England was famous for its beef, veal appeared just as frequently on the tables of England as it did in other parts of Europe. Daniel Defoe, the English journalist and author of *Robinson Crusoe*, undertook and wrote about an extensive *Tour Thro' the Whole Island of Great Britain*, published in 1724–27. In the grain-producing area around Witham in Essex, he wrote, 'their chief business is the breeding of calves…the best and fattest and the largest veal in England, if not in the world,' much of which supplied the London market. He enjoyed a loin of veal, the flesh of which was 'exceeding white and fat'.

By the seventeenth century, veal was no longer the preserve of the very wealthy – at least in the cities of northern Europe. England's famous diarist Samuel Pepys often recorded what he ate and drank. In his diary entry for 7 September 1663 he notes that he went alone to a tavern in the City of London and ate 'a chopp of veale and some bread, cheese and beer' for a shilling. Oliver Cromwell, who ruled England from 1653 to 1659 after the execution of Charles I, was reported to enjoy loin of veal with oranges and Scotch collops of veal.

Despite their name, Scotch collops are neither Scottish nor related to the word escalope. Collop derives from an old Scandinavian word for coal – presumably referring to meat that was cooked over coals – and came to mean a slice of meat, often, but not necessarily, veal. The slices were 'scotched', or beaten with the side of a knife, to flatten them before cooking. Many of the historical recipes for collops of veal that appear in British and American cookbooks sound surprisingly modern: Sir Kenelm Digby's 1669 version is served with a squeeze of orange juice, and Martha Washington's version from the 1750s uses lemon, capers and anchovies.

While English and American cookbooks of the seventeenth and eighteenth centuries were generally aimed at the domestic household, the influence of professional French chefs was never far away. French fashions waxed and waned in popularity, but aspiring English families were keen to present their guests with a blanquette, fricandeau, fricassée or ragoût of veal. At the beginning of the nineteenth century, the great French chef Carême joined the household of England's extravagant Prince Regent. A magnificent banquet held at the Brighton Pavilion in 1817 is described in Reay Tannahill's highly readable *Food in History* (1988). A hundred different dishes were served, many of which sound quite delicious, including *noix de veau à la jardinière* (rump of veal with fresh vegetables), pheasant with truffles, and chocolate soufflé. Carême returned to France in 1818, bemoaning the lack of imagination in English cooking – a reputation that remained until the late twentieth century.

Mrs Beeton certainly aimed her *Book of Household Management* (1861) at the everyday cook. It contains more than 50 recipes for veal (including calf's head, feet, knuckle, liver and sweetbreads), and she also recounts an anecdote of 'A Very Veal Dinner':

At a dinner given by Lord Polkemmet, a Scotch nobleman and judge, his guests saw, when the covers were removed, that the fare consisted of veal broth, a roasted fillet of veal, veal cutlets, a veal pie, a calf's head and calf's foot jelly. The judge, observing the surprise of his guests, volunteered an explanation – 'Ou, ay, it's a cauf; when we kill a beast, we just eat up ae side and down the tither'.

Veal remained part of the middle-class British cook's repertoire up until the Second World War. *Eating for Victory* (2007), Jill Norman's compilation of Ministry of Food leaflets, shows that veal – alongside beef, lamb and pork – was just another meat to be eked out in stews, slow roasts and savoury meat pudding. Post-war rationing made it seem wasteful to kill young animals, when there was plenty of grazing to rear cattle, and this made it more expensive. However, in *Less than Angels* (1955) the novelist Barbara Pym, writing about the middle-class households she knew, has Mabel 'staying behind to cook the Sunday joint, a fine fillet of veal.'

Meanwhile, on the other side of the Atlantic, a very fresh-sounding recipe for veal cutlets, coated in egg and breadcrumbs seasoned with lemon and marjoram, quickly fried and garnished with parsley, is given in Eliza Leslie's *Directions for Cookery*, a best-selling American cookbook first published in 1837, which gives numerous recipes for veal. Throughout the nineteenth century a steady stream of Italian, German and other European immigrants entered the US, bringing their recipes for scaloppine and schnitzels. Other variations have sprung up: veal parmigiana is an Italian-American dish combining breaded veal escalopes with tomato sauce.

In continental Europe, strongholds of the dairy industry such as the Netherlands, Switzerland and northern Italy are likely to have good veal (from the male calves) rather than good beef. In Normandy, known for its butter, cream, cheese, apples and veal, cattle grazed in the apple orchards. Veal tripe is used to make France's famous *tripes à la mode de Caen*, a speciality of Normandy.

The Netherlands has numerous recipes using veal and calves' liver. Two iconic Dutch snacks, *kalfskroketten* (which are cylindrical in shape) and *bitterballen* (round), are sold at street stalls and as

'Tripe a la Mode de Caen', a postcard from a French school in praise of the traditional classic Normandy dish, (19th century).

582 A⫯D   **Les Tripes à la Mode de Caen**

J'ai visité le Louvre et les Tuileries,
Ous que l'on vé dé statues tout du long;
J'ai visité l'Musée d'artillerie,
Mais rien ne vaut l'bieau pot de Noron !!!
Ous que l'on cuit les tripes,
Faites z à sa mode de Caen.
V'là quels sont les principes,
D'un cœur vraiement Normand :
N'y-ac qu'les tripes-z à la mode de Caen.

Qu'ma canchon dans vos cœurs trouve [sa plache
Car cha m'vexrait d'vo avoir embêté
S'rais bien heureuse d'l'y voir trouver [grâce
Car cha m'prouverait qu'vous auriez [goûte !
A c'qu'on appelle les tripes,
Faites z-à la mode de Caen.

bar snacks. The breaded croquettes are deep-fried, giving a crisp, golden exterior with a creamy veal filling – although the Dutch often joke about mysterious other meats being used.

The Swiss love veal. One claimant to the title of national dish is *Zürcher Geschnetzeltes* (called *Züri-Gschnätzlets* by the locals), a speciality of Zürich now found around the country. It is made from strips of veal cooked in a creamy white wine sauce.

Northern Italy is the home of some of the best-known of all veal dishes, made from escalopes beaten out thinly. Saltimbocca – meaning 'jump into the mouth', perhaps a description of the tastiness of the dish – combines thin slices of veal with prosciutto and a sage leaf. For *uccelli scappati* (flown-away birds) and *uccelleti falsi* (fool's birds) the veal is rolled around pancetta or prosciutto and sage.

Variations on the simple pan-fried escalopes or scaloppine include veal Marsala, in which the pan is deglazed with the rich Sicilian fortified wine, and veal piccata (also known as *scaloppine al limone*), made with lemon juice and parsley, and sometimes capers. For *scaloppine alla pizzaiola* the sauce is made with tomatoes, oregano and capers.

The Valle d'Aosta region in the mountains of north-west Italy gives its name to veal Valdostana – a breaded veal chop stuffed with prosciutto and the region's fontina cheese. Veal Cordon Bleu is similar, stuffed with ham and Gruyère cheese.

In Italy, there is a subtle distinction between *costoletta alla Milanese* and *cotoletta alla Milanese*. *Costoletta alla Milanese* is a veal chop on the bone, coated in egg and breadcrumbs and pan-fried in butter. A *cotoletta* is a boneless slice of veal (or chicken or turkey) like an escalope. More confusion awaits, as there is often heated debate about the difference between the *costoletta alla Milanese* and the Austrian Wiener Schnitzel, a veal chop or escalope coated in egg and breadcrumbs. The Viennese dredge their veal in both flour and breadcrumbs, whereas the Milanese use only breadcrumbs, and the Viennese pan-fry in lard whereas the Milanese use butter.

The authentic Austrian Wiener Schnitzel ('Viennese slice) should be made only from veal, but pork is used in other countries. It is usually served with a wedge of lemon. A variation known as veal Holstein adds anchovies, capers and a fried egg.

Slow-cooked veal

The less tender parts of the animal challenge the cook to use cooking methods and sauces that emphasize the qualities of the meat. Neck, shoulder, breast, knuckle and shin all respond well to braising, stewing and pot-roasting. Diced or minced, these cuts also make excellent pies and pâtés, meatballs, sausages and stuffings.

Many of the simplest and best slow-cooked veal dishes originate in northern and central Italy but are now found throughout the country, often adapted to make use of local herbs and vegetables. *Arrosto di vitello* is a good example, a pot roast of topside (top round) or shoulder that is part of every family's repertoire, with many regional variations. Another dish that makes good use of a tough part of the animal is *stinco*, or *schinco*, braised shin (shank) of veal. Again, there are many versions, not only in Italy but also in France, where it is called *jarret de veau*.

The best-known way of cooking shin (shank) of veal is the world-famous Milanese dish *osso buco* ('bone with a hole'), in which the shin is sawn into slices about 4 cm/1½ in thick, revealing the hollow bone filled with marrow. The slices are braised in white wine with diced vegetables; after long, slow cooking the marrow in the centre of the bones becomes meltingly tender and is traditionally eaten with a special narrow marrow spoon. The origins of the dish are buried in history, although some researchers believe it dates only from the nineteenth century. It does not appear in the anonymous *La vera cucina lombarda* (The real food of Lombardy), published in 1890. However, it is included in Pellegrino Artusi's *La scienza in cucina e l'arte di mangiar bene* (Science in the kitchen and the art of eating well), published in 1891. This was a collection of well-known recipes from all over Italy, and therefore suggests that *osso buco* was already popular. Italian food writer Anna Del Conte, who was born and raised in Milan, says that the true *osso buco* does not contain tomatoes, because 'no tomatoes used to grow in these most northerly regions of Italy'.

The summery dish of *vitello tonnato*, cold veal with a sauce of canned tuna, anchovies and capers, is a speciality of Piedmont and Lombardy in north-west Italy. Today it is made with canned tuna, but some Piedmontese claim that earlier versions were made with tuna preserved in oil, a technique that predates canning.

Many French veal dishes have aristocratic origins, dating back to the seventeenth and eighteenth centuries. White was considered an elegant colour, and master chef François Marin is thought to have devised the all-white *blanquette de veau*; the recipe first appeared in his book *Les Dons de Comus* (1739). In this classic dish, veal, onions and mushrooms are 'blanketed' in a creamy white sauce. The words 'blanquette' and 'blanket' have the same root: blanket was first used in medieval England to mean undyed woollen cloth and derives from the French word for 'white'. Marin is also credited with inventing sauce Soubise, a white sauce made by adding puréed onions to Béchamel sauce; sauce Soubise is an essential part of veal Orloff, a classic of French cuisine which was created for Prince Orloff, a nineteenth-century Russian ambassador to France.

A more down-to-earth version of veal with onions is mentioned in Mrs Maria Rundell's *A new system of domestic cookery*; first published in 1806, it became a best-seller in Britain and the US. One of her menus includes scrag of veal smothered with onions, served with broccoli and mashed potatoes 'trimmed with bacon'.

The less tender cuts of veal also come into their own when minced (ground). Many of France's terrines and pâtés and Italy's meatballs include veal, and it is a key ingredient of the traditional Bavarian sausage, *Weisswurst*, and the French *boudin blanc*.

Elaborate veal pies, eaten hot or cold, have appeared on the tables of European nobility for centuries. Made with diced or minced veal, there are many variations. English-language recipes often call for 'pie veal' – cubed, boneless pieces from the leg, shoulder or neck. Martha Bradley, in *The British Housewife* (1756), gives a recipe for veal pie seasoned with cinnamon. Later versions often combine diced and minced veal and ham with hard-boiled eggs, giving a layered or marbled effect when sliced. Legend has it that when Britain's Prime Minister William Pitt died in 1806, his last words were 'I think I could eat one of Bellamy's veal pies.'

The veal deal

Eating veal is still controversial. Many of us are haunted by images of adorable calves being shipped, weak and wobbly, in overcrowded trucks, to distant factory farms where they are raised in veal crates – narrow boxes in which they are confined without room to turn, to be fed only milk formula food, in order to keep the flesh creamy-white.

After these images were first shown in the 1970s and 80s, veal sales (at least in some countries) nose-dived. It is only relatively recently that farmers have begun to address the concerns of their customers, as animal welfare has increasingly become a consumer issue.

But there's another side to the veal question. Do you drink milk? Do you like butter, yogurt or cheese? If so, then why don't you eat veal? Veal is usually the meat of a male dairy calf. Dairy cows must give birth once a year in order to produce milk. Approximately half the calves are male, so what happens to them? Many of them are killed at one or two days old because dairy farmers are not set up to raise animals for meat. A sad waste of life, but what are the alternatives? Some calves are sold on to another farmer – often in another country – to produce white, milk-fed veal, in conditions that are far from ideal in terms of animal welfare. So, assuming we are not going to stop using dairy products, is there an 'ethical' alternative?

Rose veal is an initiative that has been led by the UK. The government banned veal crates in 1990. Then the country was badly hit by BSE ('mad cow disease'), and the EU imposed a ten-year ban on British beef exports. Unable to export their unwanted male calves, dairy farmers were left with a stark choice: kill them or (find someone else to) raise them for veal. British farmers are legally required to give calves space to move around, bedding to lie in and a nutritionally balanced diet that includes grain and/or forage: the calves' muscles and digestive systems develop more naturally than crate-raised, exclusively milk-fed animals and the result is darker pink meat with a subtle beefy flavour.

The calves are generally slaughtered at six to eight months old (most of the lamb and pork we eat is killed at five to six months). But of the 500,000 bull dairy calves born in the UK each year, less than 1 per cent are currently reared for veal. In January 2012 an RSPCA spokesman urged British consumers to eat British rose veal: 'If you don't, there's no market for the farmer and the calves will be killed or sent abroad.'

In nature, calves remain with their mothers, suckling for about nine months, but they start to nibble grass at an early age and are soon on a mixed diet of milk and pasture. Since ancient times man has devised techniques to keep veal flesh pale and delicate, including keeping calves tethered in a stall and feeding them only on milk. Over the past 50 years, dairy cows and veal, pigs, chickens and other animals have been intensively reared (factory-farmed) to keep costs down. Yet while many consumers associate veal with cruelty, they regularly tuck into chicken or bacon and eggs.

Veal crates became illegal in the UK in 1990 and have been banned in the European Union since 2007. Switzerland, with its substantial dairy industry, continues to use crates. In the US, some states have already banned veal crates and the American Veal Association plans to phase out the use of crates by 2017.

However, as with most farmed animals, there are many options when it comes to rearing veal calves, whether for white (milk-fed) veal or rose (red or grain-fed) veal. Depending on the country and the scale of the operation, calves may be housed indoors, without daylight, on slatted floors, with little or no bedding, in cramped conditions. Better farms keep the calves in small groups in light, airy barns with plenty of clean straw bedding and plenty of room to frisk and play.

When buying veal, look for labels of approval from animal welfare organizations such as CIWF (Compassion in World Farming). Organic meat is also likely to be raised more humanely.

White (milk-fed) veal is prized for its creamy-white or very pale pink flesh. The calves are fed almost exclusively on milk formula, which keeps the flesh pale. This is still the most widely produced type of veal throughout Europe and North America: the restaurant trade demands pale meat and in many countries, including France, Italy, the Netherlands, Germany, Austria and Switzerland, milk-fed veal has never been off the menu. In Italian, *vitello* is young, milk-fed veal and *vitellone* is darker meat from an older animal. Around six million calves are reared for veal within the EU every year, the biggest producers being France, the Netherlands and Italy.

The great majority of milk-fed veal comes from bull calves not needed in dairy herds, mainly the instantly recognizable black and white Holstein-Friesian cattle. Following changes to EU regulations, their diet now includes a small amount of fibrous feed and iron, to enable their digestive systems to develop normally and prevent them from becoming weak and anaemic. The calves are generally slaughtered at five to seven months old.

Another tradition is being developed commercially on small to medium-sized farms in South-West France. Using a beef breed such as Limousin, Charolais or Blonde d'Aquitaine (or a dairy-beef crossbreed), the calves are suckled twice a day by their own mothers. The cows' diet is monitored to make sure their milk is as nutritious as possible and the calves are given small amounts of solid food. The calves reach optimum weight at four to five months old. This milk-fed veal (*veau sous la mère*, meaning 'under the mother') is renowned for its delicately textured, very pale pink flesh and is meltingly tender when cooked. It commands a high price and is sold with a Label Rouge, an official French guarantee of superior quality.

Rose, rosé or grain-fed veal is rosy pink in colour and has a subtle beefy taste. Calves are generally reared to be heavier than for white veal and are usually slaughtered at six to eight months. Young bulls of eight to eleven months can be sold as 'baby beef'. Calves may be raised by their mothers or fed milk formula and weaned at six to eight weeks; after that their diet may include milk, forage, grain and/or concentrates.

Rose veal comes from the male calves of dairy cows. The commonest dairy cows in Europe and North America are Holstein-Friesians, but even specialized dairy breeds such as Guernseys and Jerseys may be reared as rose veal. Rose veal in the UK is raised to high welfare standards, and producers in other countries are increasingly looking to improve conditions. In Spain, calves are generally slaughtered at nine to twelve months old; the resulting dark pink veal is known as *ternera* – effectively it is young beef – and it is more common in Spain than older beef.

From a welfare point of view the best type of 'rose' veal is **free-raised, pasture-raised or grass-fed veal**. As in the days before factory farming, calves are reared on pasture alongside their mothers, where they are free to suckle and nibble grass. The age at which these calves are killed varies, generally between three and six months, and the meat is deep pink and often lower in fat than other types of veal. This method is preferred by organic farmers. Although not widespread, it is found in various countries, including the UK, France, Italy and the US.

Rose veal is supported by Compassion in World Farming (CIWF), as long as the calves are reared to high welfare standards: either outdoors with the mother or indoors with a small group of other calves with plenty of space, straw bedding and adequate nutrition.

ESCALOPES

Escalopes of veal, or *scaloppine* in Italian, are probably the first things that come to mind when we think of veal. However, whereas in the past they were often rather bland and needed a powerful sauce, today's animal-welfare-conscious rose veal has much more flavour – better to enhance that flavour rather than overwhelm it.

The best escalopes traditionally come from the leg, and weigh approximately 125 g/4½ oz. Look for pieces cut from a single piece of muscle, without any tendons. They should be thin and evenly sliced, about 5 mm/¼ in thick. If you have thicker or uneven slices, place them between two pieces of clingfilm (plastic wrap) and beat with a rolling pin to flatten them as thinly as you can.

Preparing escalopes

There are three main ways to prepare escalopes for pan-frying:

1. Plain Pat the escalopes dry on both sides with kitchen paper, then season with salt and pepper.

2. Floured Dry the escalopes and then lightly dust with seasoned plain (all-purpose) flour. Shake off any excess. The thin coating of flour helps to give colour to the escalopes and thickens the sauce.

3. Breadcrumbed Dry the escalopes. Dust lightly but evenly with seasoned flour, then dip in egg wash (beat an egg in a bowl with 1–2 tsp water) and finally in a bowl of fine fresh breadcrumbs. When pan-fried in hot oil or butter, this gives a crunchy coating. This is effectively the classic Austrian dish, Wiener Schnitzel, served simply with a squeeze of lemon juice.

Cooking escalopes

For all three methods you need a hot, heavy-bottomed frying pan (skillet). Add 1–2 tsp olive oil and 1 tsp butter and then, as the butter melts and fizzles, add the escalopes. Brown lightly on one side and then turn over and brown on the other – they should be golden and not dark brown – the whole process will take 2–3 minutes on each side.

Saltimbocca

In Italian, this means 'to jump in the mouth'. The essence is of simplicity and freshness: veal, sage, prosciutto and lemon juice, nothing more.

4 veal escalopes, 125 g/4½ oz each, cut in half
salt and pepper
4 slices of prosciutto
8 sage leaves
juice of 1 or 2 lemons

Prepare and cook the escalopes as in method 1. Place a half escalope on each of 4 warmed plates. Place a slice of prosciutto and 2 sage leaves on each one and put the other half escalope on top.

Return the pan to a high heat and add the lemon juice, swirl to take up the pan juices and pour over the veal. Excellent with creamy mashed potatoes and spinach.

Scaloppine al limone

The freshness of the lemon brings out the sweetness of the meat.

4 veal escalopes, 125 g/4½ oz each
2–3 tbsp seasoned flour
150 ml/5 fl oz/⅔ cup dry white wine
juice of 2 lemons
55 g/2 oz/4 tbsp butter
1 tbsp chopped flat-leaf parsley
matchsticks of blanched lemon zest (optional)

Prepare and cook the escalopes as in method 2. Remove from the pan and keep warm. Return the pan to the heat, pour in the white wine and boil to reduce to about 2 tbsp. Add the lemon juice and reduce by half, then take the pan off the heat and swirl in the butter and parsley. Return the veal to the pan along with any juices and coat in the sauce. Serve immediately, with green beans, courgettes (zucchini) and blanched lemon zest, if you like.

Scaloppine al Marsala

Marsala is a fortified wine from Sicily; it gained wider fame in the eighteenth century when the Sicilians substituted their own wine for rum on British naval vessels. Use a dry Marsala for this dish – but if you have only sweet Marsala, for making zabaglione, then no matter, it will do fine!

4 veal escalopes, 125 g/4½ oz each
2–3 tbsp seasoned flour
125 ml/4 fl oz/½ cup Marsala
55 g/2 oz/4 tbsp butter

Prepare and cook the escalopes as in method 2. Remove from the pan and keep warm. Pour the Marsala into the pan, let it bubble up and reduce by half, stirring well, then take the pan off the heat and swirl in the butter to create a sauce. Pour over the escalopes and serve immediately, with green beans.

Escalopes with cheese & ham

Variations of this dish are found in Italy, Austria and Switzerland. You can use either cooked ham or cured ham (such as prosciutto) and any good melting cheese, such as Emmental, Gruyère or Edam.

SERVES 4

8 x 85 g/3 oz veal escalopes
salt and pepper
4 thin slices of ham
4 thin slices of cheese
2–3 tbsp seasoned flour
1 egg, beaten in a shallow
  bowl with 1–2 tsp water
about 85 g/3 oz/2 cups fine
  fresh breadcrumbs
lemon wedges, to serve

Make sure the escalopes are very thin; if necessary beat them between two pieces of clingfilm (plastic wrap), using a rolling pin, but take care not to make any holes or tears in the meat.

Place 4 escalopes on a tray and season lightly. Place the ham and cheese slices on top, leaving a small border all round. Brush the border with the beaten egg, then place the other 4 escalopes on top and press the edges together to seal the two pieces of meat together well – without any ham or cheese sticking out.

Proceed as in method 3 (see page 217) and cook until golden and crisp all over; when you cut them, the cheese should be very melty.

Serve with lemon wedges, watercress and new potatoes.

Paupiettes

These are usually veal escalopes filled with a stuffing and then gently braised, with a sauce made from the ensuing juices. With today's flavoursome veal, you need to think about flavour marriage, not flavour takeover. This elegant dish is based on some of my favourite veal bedfellows: mushrooms, rosemary and lemon.

SERVES 4

8 thin veal escalopes,
  about 85 g/3 oz each
1 tbsp olive oil
1 shallot, finely chopped
100 ml/3½ fl oz/6 tbsp
  dry vermouth
100 ml/3½ fl oz/6 tbsp
  veal stock
juice of 1 lemon
2 tbsp double (heavy)
  cream

MUSHROOM STUFFING
225 g/8 oz firm white
  mushrooms
2 tsp fresh rosemary
1 tbsp chopped flat-leaf
  parsley
1 shallot, finely chopped
grated zest of 1 lemon
a little truffle oil (optional)
salt and pepper

To make the stuffing, blitz the mushrooms in a food processor – do a few at a time to make sure you get a rough chop and not a purée. You can chop the rosemary and parsley in the machine at the same time. Mix with the shallot and lemon zest and a few drops of truffle oil, if using. Season lightly.

Make sure the escalopes are very thin; if necessary beat them between two pieces of clingfilm (plastic wrap), using a rolling pin, but take care not to make any holes or tears. Divide the stuffing among the paupiettes, then roll them up and tie with string, around the middle and end to end to make sure they don't fall apart. It is traditional to secure them with cocktail sticks, but I think string holds them together better and makes them easier to cook.

Heat the olive oil in a pan with a well-fitting lid, just large enough to hold the paupiettes in one layer. Brown the paupiettes all over in the oil, then reduce the heat to very low, cover with a cartouche (a disc of greaseproof/wax paper that fits snugly in the pan), put on the lid and cook gently for about 20 minutes. Alternatively cook in a preheated oven at 160°C/325°F/gas 3. They are ready when you can easily pierce them with a skewer. Remove from the pan, cover and leave to rest in a warm place.

Return the pan to a low heat and add the chopped shallot, stirring to soften and pick up the juices. Pour in the vermouth and reduce by half, then add the stock, bring to a simmer and add the lemon juice and cream. Reduce until slightly thickened.

Cut each paupiette into thin slices. Pour a little sauce onto each plate and arrange the sliced paupiettes, two per person, on top.

Tip

Try adding chopped sorrel to the sauce instead of lemon juice: the astringent flavour marries well with the veal.

Medallions of veal with capers & parsley

I love the simplicity of this, the freshness of the herb with the tang of the capers (I know, I *love* capers), but it's also great with the addition of small black olives, or some grated lemon zest and lemon juice.

SERVES 4

4 medallions of veal,
  about 150 g/5 oz each
salt and pepper
1 tbsp olive oil
1 tbsp butter
1 small onion, finely
  chopped
2 tsp capers, rinsed
2 tbsp chopped fresh
  parsley

You need a heavy-bottomed pan into which all the meat can go at once without being crowded. Dry the veal medallions on kitchen paper and season with salt and pepper.

Put the pan over a high heat, add the olive oil and when very hot place the medallions carefully and firmly in the pan. Cook for about 3 minutes until lightly browned, turn and brown on the other side for 3 minutes, then lower the heat and cook more gently for another 3 minutes. Remove the medallions from the pan and leave to rest in a warm place.

Add the butter to the pan and then add the chopped onion, stir to absorb the meat juices and cook until lightly coloured. Add 4 tbsp water, stir in the capers and parsley, and reduce to make a light sauce. Tip any juices from the medallions into the pan and stir in, check for seasoning and serve over the meat. It goes really well with a chunk of polenta.

Tip

If you like, add 1 tsp mustard after the onions have browned, and stir in before you add the water.

Grilled veal cutlets

By these I mean cuts still on the bone. A cutlet is usually from the best end of neck and a chop from the loin, but the size will vary, depending on the age and breed of the animal. The best way to cook them is on a hot grill or griddle pan; this way the heat gets to the bone quickly and the meat is almost caramelized on both sides; you can then continue at a lower temperature if the chops are not cooked through: either reduce the heat under the pan or bring the veal to the edge of the grill.

4 veal cutlets or chops
salt and pepper
a little olive oil

Heat a grill or griddle pan until smoking hot. Dry the veal on kitchen paper, season lightly with salt and pepper and rub in a little olive oil. Press down in the hot pan and sear on one side, don't move it for about 3 minutes, then turn over and repeat on the other side; the surface should have a lovely brown crust. Using tongs, cook for 2 minutes on the fat side and, lastly, cook on the bone itself. Leave to rest for a few minutes. The meat should be a lovely pink inside, moist and sweet.

Serve with béarnaise sauce (see page 55) or with roasted red peppers, skinned and sliced: the sweetness of the peppers makes a great marriage with the grilled meat.

See picture overleaf (LEFT: grilled cutlets with a lemon and parsley crust; RIGHT: simply grilled)

Cutlets with ginger & lime

Almost but not quite a sauce, and I can never decide whether to serve this on top of the cutlets or to the side. Perhaps on the side, then you get the full flavour of the lovely brown crust on the veal.

55 g/2 oz fresh ginger, peeled
1 lime
1 tsp olive oil
2 shallots, finely chopped
1 tsp caster (superfine) sugar
250 ml/9 fl oz/1 cup single (light) cream
salt and pepper
4 veal cutlets or chops, about 200 g/7 oz each

Slice the ginger thinly and then cut into thin matchsticks; set aside. Peel the lime in very thin strips, blanch the strips in boiling water for 1 minute, then refresh in cold water and set aside.

Heat the olive oil in a small pan and soften the shallots for a few minutes. Add the ginger and the sugar and stir to caramelize lightly. Add the lime peel and the cream and cook until you have a spoonable mixture. Add a squeeze of lime juice and season to taste.

Meanwhile, cook the veal on a hot grill or griddle pan (see opposite). Serve with the ginger cream.

Cutlets with a lemon & parsley crust

70 g/2½ oz unsmoked streaky bacon
handful of fresh parsley
1 tsp chopped fresh rosemary
grated zest of 2 lemons and juice of ½ lemon
black pepper
4 veal cutlets or chops, about 200 g/7 oz each
1 tsp olive oil
2 tsp butter

In a food processor, blitz the bacon, parsley, rosemary, lemon zest and juice and pepper together to form a spreadable mixture. Dry the cutlets on kitchen paper and press the mixture evenly over both sides of the cutlets.

Preheat the oven to 180°C/350°F/gas 4. Heat a heavy-bottomed frying pan (skillet) with an ovenproof handle over a medium-high heat. Add the oil and butter; when the butter starts to fizzle, place the cutlets in the pan and cook for about 5 minutes, until the crust is lightly coloured. Turn carefully and put the pan in the oven for about 10 minutes to cook through. Serve hot.

ROASTING VEAL

Veal is much leaner than beef and has not got the fat to protect it and keep it moist during long cooking. Even prime cuts such as loin and rump (top round) are best cooked with a little water or wine to keep them moist. I often use a recipe for a loin of veal (or pork) that is smothered in a mixture of mustard and butter and basted with dry vermouth and stock, which really keeps in the moisture and makes a delicious sauce.

As with all cuts of meat, make sure that your veal is at room temperature before you cook it: a large joint will need to be out of the fridge for a good hour. The difference of 5 degrees or so reduces the cooking time and also lessens the likelihood of dry meat. Always remove meat from a vacuum pack at least 30 minutes before cooking, to allow air to get to the meat, open up the pores and improve the flavour.

Roast rump of veal with spring vegetables

Here is a lovely dish making delicious use of the juices from the roasted veal. Serve the veal sliced over the dish of vegetables.

SERVES 4

700 g/1 lb 9 oz rump (top round) of veal, or boned loin
salt and pepper
3 tbsp olive oil
100 g/3½ oz meat trimmings, or unsmoked bacon
25 g/1 oz/2 tbsp butter
8 small shallots
8 small waxy potatoes, such as pink fir apple or Ratte
8 chantenay carrots or baby carrots
2 spring onions
2 garlic cloves, crushed
150 ml/5 fl oz/⅔ cup veal stock
1 tsp chopped chervil

Preheat the oven to 200°C/400°F/gas 6. Season the veal with salt and pepper. Heat 1 tbsp olive oil in a small roasting pan and brown the veal all over. Add the trimmings or bacon and the butter and cook in the oven for about 20 minutes, basting occasionally with the buttery juices.

Reduce the oven temperature to 150°C/300°F/gas 2 and cook for a further 40 minutes, until the juices run pale pink when pierced with a skewer, or the internal temperature is 50°C/120°F on a meat thermometer. Remove the veal from the pan, cover with foil and leave to rest in a warm place.

Heat the remaining 2 tbsp olive oil in a heavy-bottomed pan, add the shallots and potatoes and cook over a medium heat, stirring or shaking the pan from time to time until lightly coloured. Add the carrots, spring onions and garlic, shake to coat them in the juices, reduce the heat, cover and cook gently until just done. The carrots should still have some 'bite'. Season to taste, transfer the vegetables to a warmed serving dish and keep warm.

Put the roasting pan over a medium-high heat, add the stock and reduce by half stirring to incorporate any residue. Strain into a serving jug. Slice the veal and serve over the vegetables. Spoon a tablespoon or two of the reduced juices over the veal and sprinkle with chopped chervil.

Italian roast veal

This recipe is designed for a prime cut, such as the leg or loin, that needs little cooking and remains moist and slightly pink; it needs to be one piece and not a boned joint. A smallish joint, as here, can be cooked on the hob for the whole time, or part of the cooking can be done in an oven. You can use a pan with a lid (Dutch oven) or a deep frying pan with foil to cover.

When I was developing this recipe, my wife found an aubergine in the fridge needing to be used, so she made caponata, which, with its addition of anchovies, went very well with the veal.

SERVES 4–6

700–900 g/1½–2 lb piece
 of veal
salt and pepper
2 tbsp groundnut
 (peanut) oil
1 large onion, halved
 and sliced
3 garlic cloves, crushed
2 large ripe tomatoes,
 roughly chopped
sprig of thyme
2 bay leaves
125 ml/4 fl oz/½ cup
 dry white wine

Dry the meat thoroughly and season with salt and pepper. Heat the oil in the pan over a high heat, add the meat and brown it all over; this will take about 5 minutes. Lower the heat and add the onion, stirring in among the meat juices until lightly coloured and softened, about 10 minutes, turning the veal occasionally. Now add the garlic and stir gently to infuse its flavours, then add the tomatoes and crush with a wooden spoon to start the juices oozing out. Add the herbs and wine, bring to a simmer and turn the meat over.

Cover with a lid or foil and, if cooking on the hob, turn the heat to low and cook for 10 minutes, then turn the meat and cook for another 20 minutes. If cooking in the oven, it should be preheated to 110°C/225°F/gas ¼; cook the meat for 30 minutes, turning once. When cooked, the temperature in the middle of the meat should measure 50°C/120°F on a meat thermometer.

Leave the meat to rest in a warm place and strain the juices into another pan, pushing through as much of the tomato and onion as you can, to create a sauce. Season to taste. Slice the meat quite thinly and serve with a little sauce. Delicious with a creamy mash or with caponata (recipe overleaf).

Caponata

A delicious recipe from Sicily, with really robust flavours. I have seen some recipes that add harissa, the North African chilli paste – not strictly authentic but if you like spice, it works well. Caponata can be eaten on its own or as a side dish, especially with barbecues. It improves with keeping for a day or two; reheat gently before serving.

SERVES 4

90 ml/6 tbsp olive oil
75 ml/5 tbsp red wine
  vinegar
85 g/3 oz/scant ½ cup soft
  brown sugar
3 tbsp tomato purée
4 celery stalks, cut in
  chunks
1 red onion, chopped
370 g/13 oz cherry
  tomatoes
700 g/1 lb 9 oz aubergines
  (eggplants), cut into
  cubes
2 tbsp sultanas (golden
  raisins)
2 tbsp capers, rinsed,
  or caperberries
55 g/2 oz can anchovies,
  drained and chopped
125 g/4½ oz olives, pitted
  and halved
25 g/1 oz pine nuts, toasted
2–3 tbsp chopped flat-leaf
  parsley

Preheat the oven to 200°C/400°F/gas 6.

Mix the oil, vinegar, sugar and tomato purée in a bowl. Add the celery, onion, tomatoes and aubergine and mix thoroughly but gently. Spread out in a roasting pan and roast for 35 minutes, until soft and beginning to brown. Remove from the oven.

Put the sultanas in a sieve and pour boiling water over them. Add the sultanas to the aubergine mixture, then add the capers, anchovies, olives and pine nuts. Serve warm, sprinkled with parsley.

Vitello tonnato

This Italian classic is often made by simmering the veal with aromatic herbs and vegetables, but I think roasting works well. You will need to start this dish a day or two before you want to serve it. I can never quite understand how a 'classic' dish can be made with canned tuna; still, I suppose it's about as old as a classic car!

SERVES 4

600 g/1 lb 5 oz rump (top round) or boned loin of veal
salt and pepper
250 ml/9 fl oz/1 cup olive oil
1 garlic clove
2 tsp capers in brine, drained, plus extra for garnish
3 anchovy fillets
200 g/7 oz canned tuna in oil, drained
2 egg yolks
juice of 1 lemon
2 tbsp chopped flat-leaf parsley

Preheat the oven to 200°C/400°F/gas 6. Season the veal with salt and pepper. Heat 1 tablespoon of the olive oil in a small roasting pan and brown the veal all over, then cook in the oven for about 20 minutes, basting occasionally.

Reduce the oven temperature to 150°C/300°F/gas 2 and cook for a further 40 minutes until the juices run pale pink when pierced with a skewer, or the internal temperature is 50°C/120°F on a meat thermometer. Remove the veal from the oven, cover with foil and leave until cold.

Pound the garlic with the capers in a pestle and mortar, then blend in the anchovies and tuna, then the egg yolks, lemon juice and 2 teaspoons of the liquid from the caper jar. Using a large whisk, gradually whisk in the olive oil until you have a rich, pourable sauce.

Slice the veal thinly. On individual plates, create a sort of lasagne with the sauce and meat, with up to three layers. It's best left to marinate for 24 hours to allow the flavours to develop. To serve, sprinkle with capers and parsley.

Pot roast veal

Many great veal dishes come from northern Italy: this is based on a family favourite known as *arrosto di vitello*.

SERVES 4–6

1 kg/2¼ lb boned rolled
  veal joint, such as topside
  (top round) or shoulder
salt and pepper
3 garlic cloves, sliced
handful of fresh flat-leaf
  parsley, roughly chopped
1–2 tbsp olive oil
1 large onion, sliced
1 celery stalk, diced
1 carrot, diced
a sprig of rosemary
1 bay leaf
100 ml/3½ fl oz/
  scant ½ cup dry
  white wine

For best results, remove the string from the veal and open it up on a board, with the skin side down. Season with salt and pepper, strew in the garlic and sprinkle on the parsley. Roll up again and tie with fresh string. If having to re-tie the meat worries you, you can skip this bit! But it is worth it.

Heat the oil in an ovenproof pan with a well-fitting lid (Dutch oven). Brown the meat all over and then remove and set aside. Reduce the heat and add the onion, celery and carrot, stirring to pick up the meat juices and to colour slightly.

Return the meat to the pan, add the rosemary and bay leaf and cover with a cartouche – a disc of greaseproof (wax) paper cut to fit snugly over the meat. Add the lid, turn the heat to very low and simmer for about 2–3 hours. Alternatively, cook it in the oven at 160°C/325°F/gas 3 for about 2–3 hours. Check occasionally: if it looks to be getting a bit dry, add some water. When cooked, the meat should be meltingly tender.

Remove the meat and leave to rest in a warm place. Add the wine to the pan and simmer for a few minutes, then push through a sieve to form a rough sauce. Taste for seasoning and serve with the sliced veal.

Osso buco

Osso buco is the Italian for bone with a hole, but these holes are full of rich, savoury marrow. Some people serve this with a lemon gremolata (see page 176 for orange gremolata), but I don't think it needs it.

SERVES 4

4 pieces of veal shin
  (shank) on the bone,
  about 5 cm/2 in thick
  (about 1–1.2 kg/
  2¼–2½ lb in total)
1–2 tbsp seasoned plain
  flour
1 tbsp olive oil
40 g/1½ oz/3 tbsp butter
2 onions, coarsely chopped
2 celery stalks, coarsely
  chopped
1 large carrot, diced
2 garlic cloves, crushed
4 anchovies
strip of lemon peel
1 tsp tomato purée
200 ml/7 fl oz/generous
  ¾ cup dry white wine

Toss the veal in seasoned flour. Heat a large pan in which the veal pieces can all sit flat, add the oil and 1 tbsp butter and brown the veal on both sides over a high heat; remove and set aside.

Add the remaining butter to the pan and lightly brown the onions, celery and carrot. Add the garlic, anchovies and lemon peel and stir in the tomato purée. Place the veal on top and pour in the white wine, allow to bubble up, cover with a cartouche – a disc of greaseproof (wax) paper that fits snugly over the veal – and simmer for about 2 hours, until the meat is really tender and falling off the bone. Alternatively, cook in a preheated oven at 180°C/350°F/gas 4. Serve hot, with risotto Milanese (recipe overleaf).

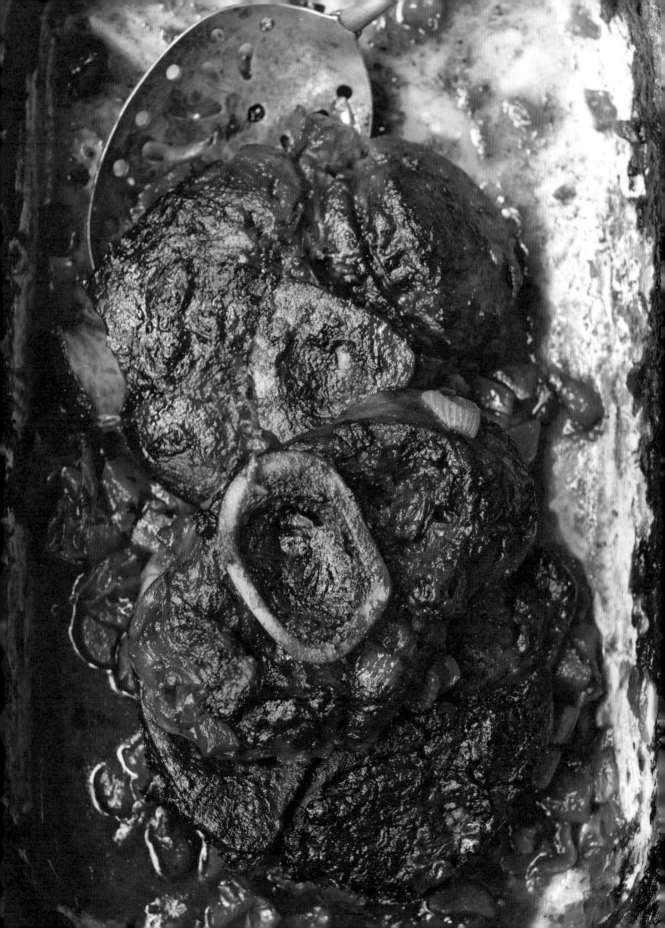

Risotto Milanese

This golden, saffron-scented risotto is the traditional accompaniment to osso buco, seen on the opposite page, served with lentils.

SERVES 4

1 litre/1¾ pints/4 cups
  chicken stock
1 tbsp butter
1 onion, finely chopped
285 g/10 oz/scant 1½ cups
  arborio or carnaroli
  (risotto) rice
½ tsp saffron threads
125 ml/4 fl oz/½ cup dry
  white wine
1 tbsp olive oil
55 g/2 oz Parmesan, grated
salt and black pepper

Heat the stock to boiling point and keep it just simmering. In a wide, heavy-bottomed pan over a medium heat, melt the butter and soften the onion. Add the rice and stir well to coat in the butter, sprinkle in the saffron, stirring to release its flavours, then add the wine and stir until it has been absorbed.

Now begin to add the stock, a ladleful at a time, stirring constantly and making sure that the liquid is all absorbed before adding the next ladleful. After about 25 minutes the rice should be tender but still firm to bite; the more you stir, the creamier it will become! You may not need all the stock. Take off the heat and stir, in the olive oil and cheese and serve immediately.

Slow-cooked shoulder of veal

Bacon, thyme and mushrooms combine beautifully with veal; the juices create a sauce and also help to keep the meat moist.

SERVES 6–8

1.5 kg/3½ lb boned rolled shoulder of veal
salt and pepper
85 g/3 oz unsmoked bacon lardons
85 g/3 oz/6 tbsp butter
sprig of thyme
350 g/12 oz small button mushrooms
20 small shallots or baby onions, peeled (see tip, page 109)
125 ml/4 fl oz/1 cup dry white wine

Heat the oven to 160°C/325°F/gas 3.

Season the veal with salt and pepper. Heat a large ovenproof pan or casserole with a well-fitting lid (Dutch oven). Brown the bacon in 55 g/2 oz/ 4 tbsp of the butter, then add the veal and brown all over. Throw in the thyme, cover and cook in the oven for 2–3 hours, turning and basting the meat occasionally.

About 30 minutes before the end of the cooking time, cook the mushrooms in the remaining butter in a pan over a high heat; remove with a slotted spoon and set aside. Add the shallots or onions to the pan and brown lightly, then add them to the veal for the last 30 minutes or so of cooking.

When the veal is very tender, remove from the casserole and leave to rest in a warm place. Add the mushrooms and the wine to the casserole and place over a medium-high heat to reduce slightly. Season to taste and serve with the sliced veal. The sauce is thin but full of flavour.

Veal stew with rosemary

This recipe is for any diced veal – shoulder, breast or trimmings from other cuts – the more gelatinous, the better.

SERVES 4

1 tbsp olive oil
700–800 g/1^{1}/$_2$–1^3/$_4$ lb
  veal, diced into 2 cm/^{3}/$_4$ in
  chunks
salt and pepper
1 onion, diced
1 leek, sliced down the
  middle and then diced
3 carrots, cut into batons
  or thick slices at an angle
3 tsp tomato purée
1 bay leaf
2 sprigs of rosemary
100 ml/3^1/$_2$ fl oz/
  scant ^{1}/$_2$ cup dry
  white wine
water or stock
2 tbsp chopped fresh
  parsley

Preheat the oven to 150°C/300°F/gas 2.

Heat a large ovenproof pan or casserole with a well-fitting lid (Dutch oven); add the olive oil. Dry the veal pieces thoroughly on kitchen paper and season lightly, then brown in the hot pan – do this in batches to make sure the meat is properly seared. Remove the meat from the pan and set aside.

Add the onion to the pan, stirring to scrape up the juices and to lightly colour the onion. Add the leek and carrots, stirring gently until lightly coloured. Stir in the tomato purée and then add the herbs and wine. Return the meat to the pan and stir to mix thoroughly. Top up with just enough stock or water to cover the meat, and then cover the pan and place in the oven for about 2 hours.

When the meat is tender, remove the lid and simmer briefly to form a light sauce. Remove the bay leaf and rosemary, season to taste and add the chopped parsley. Serve hot, with polenta.

Stuffed breast of veal

This is one of those party dishes in which all the hard work is done in advance.
I recently made this for a family get-together with all my siblings and their spouses;
it meant that I had time to talk to them and still produce an interesting dish.

The basis of this idea comes from a chef whom I have admired for many years.
In his book *No Place Like Home*, Rowley Leigh stuffs his breast with pork, but
I have used bacon instead. You could, if you like, brine the veal breast (see page
252), which helps firm up the meat, but if you decide on that course make sure
it is in the brine for only a couple of days and rinse it under a cold tap and dry
thoroughly before cooking. Here, I have followed Rowley's method of marinating
the veal overnight with some herbs.

Recipe continues
overleaf

SERVES 6–10

1 veal breast, which can
  weigh between 1.5 and
  3 kg/3¹/₂–7 lb
salt and pepper
sprigs of thyme
100 g/3¹/₂ oz two-day-old
  bread
20 g/³/₄ oz fresh parsley
  leaves
370 g/13 oz unsmoked
  bacon
2 onions, finely chopped
2 tbsp olive oil
1 onion, roughly chopped
1 carrot, roughly chopped
1 head of garlic, cut in half
  horizontally
300 ml/10 fl oz/ 1¹/₄ cups
  dry white wine

Cut the bones out of the breast (and keep them for a braising base or to make a veal stock). Rub the meat with salt and rub some thyme between your hands so the leaves fall over the meat, but not the stalks. Refrigerate overnight.

In a food processor, blitz the bread with the parsley; set aside. Briefly whizz the bacon in the machine to form a rough forcemeat. Soften the finely chopped onions in 1 tbsp olive oil over a medium heat. Mix the onions with the bacon, bread and parsley and season generously.

Spread the veal on a board and spread the stuffing over it, leaving a clear border all round, so when you roll it up none of the stuffing comes out. Tie it up all the way along, so it holds its shape and doesn't fall apart during cooking.

Preheat the oven to 180°C/350°F/gas 4. In a large roasting pan over a medium heat, brown the meat in the remaining 1 tbsp olive oil. Set aside. In the same pan, brown the roughly chopped onion and carrot, adding the garlic at the last moment. Put the meat on top of the vegetables and place in the oven for 30 minutes. Pour over the white wine and baste with the juices. Reduce the oven temperature to 150°C/300°F/gas 2 and cook, basting occasionally, for another 2 hours.

Remove the meat and leave to rest. Add a little water to the pan juices, stirring to loosen any bits and then strain. Taste and season. Slice the veal and serve with the gravy, mashed potatoes and some quickly cooked green vegetables, such as spinach.

Tip

Instead of the parsley in the stuffing, try some fresh wild garlic. The gentle garlic flavour and colour work very well.

Blanquette de veau

This French bistro classic is a favourite of mine and you can vary the ingredients.
I use tarragon because it's such a good flavour with the cream sauce, but if you
have lots of parsley or even chives, use them instead. The name 'blanquette'
implies whiteness, but I have used leeks and have also seen baby carrots included,
which of course add a lovely crunch and a splash of colour. Tiny pink fir apple
potatoes are good, too.

SERVES 4

700–800 g/1½–1¾ lb
  diced veal, preferably
  from the shoulder
5 peppercorns
1 bay leaf
sprig each of thyme and
  rosemary
1 star anise
8–12 shallots or baby
  onions, peeled (see tip,
  page 109)
200 g/7 oz button
  mushrooms kept whole
  if small or quartered
25 g/1 oz/2 tbsp butter
25 g/1 oz/3 tbsp plain
  (all-purpose) flour
salt and pepper
2 tsp chopped fresh
  tarragon
grated zest of 1 lemon
2 tbsp double (heavy)
  cream

Rinse the veal with cold water and place in a heavy-bottomed pan with
a lid. Add about 500 ml/18 fl oz/2 cups cold water, just to cover the meat,
and bring just to the boil. Reduce the heat to a simmer, skim off any
foam and add the peppercorns, bay leaf, thyme, rosemary and star anise.
Cover and simmer over a low heat for about 1 hour. Add the shallots and
mushrooms and simmer for another 30 minutes or until the meat is just
tender.

Strain the stock from the veal into a large measuring jug. Melt the butter
in a saucepan until foaming but not brown, stir in the flour to form a roux
and cook, stirring, for a few minutes. Add 500 ml/18 fl oz/2 cups of the veal
stock, allow to bubble up and boil briskly to reduce slightly and intensify
the flavour. You are looking for a light coating sauce. Taste for seasoning,
add the tarragon and lemon zest, then finish with the cream. Put the
meat, mushrooms and shallots into the sauce, removing any peppercorns
and bits of herb that may be adhering. Simmer for a minute or two and
serve with pilaf rice.

Veal & ham pie

A traditional British cold pie to make ahead for lunch, supper, or a wonderful picnic treat, with chutney or another favourite condiment. It looks impressive but it's quite straightforward to make. You can use a hot water pastry crust, but I have opted for puff pastry.

SERVES 8–10

700 g/1 lb 9 oz puff pastry
450 g/1 lb cooked veal, minced
450 g/1 lb cooked ham, minced
1 onion, finely chopped
55 g/2 oz/1¼ cups fresh white breadcrumbs
1 tbsp chopped fresh chives
grated zest of 1 lemon
salt and pepper
5 hard-boiled eggs, shelled
egg wash made from 1 egg, beaten thoroughly with a little water
375 ml/13 fl oz/generous 1½ cups veal stock
3 leaves of gelatine

Lightly grease a drop-sided loaf tin, about 25 x 10 x 10 cm/10 x 4 x 4 in, or a deep cake tin with a removable base, and line with baking parchment. Cut off three-quarters of the pastry, roll out and use to line the base and sides of the tin.

Mix together the veal, ham, onion, breadcrumbs, chives and lemon zest, season well and place half in the tin, pushing down gently. Cut the ends off the boiled eggs and place in a line, end to end, in the middle of the tin, season lightly and cover with the remaining meat mixture, pressing down to make sure there are no spaces. Dampen the edges of the pastry.

Preheat the oven to 200°C/400°F/gas 6. Roll out the remaining pastry. Lift over the tin, pressing down well to seal the pastry edges. Trim and use the trimmings to decorate the top. Make a small hole in the centre of the pie. Brush with the beaten egg. Bake in the hot oven for 30 minutes, then reduce the oven temperature to 180°C/350°F/gas 4 and cook for a further 1 hour. Leave to cool.

Bring the stock to the boil and remove from the heat. Soften the gelatine in a little cold water, then dissolve in the hot stock. Leave until cold but not set.

Pour the cold stock through a funnel into the hole in the top of the pie, a little at a time; take care because it will settle slowly and you may not need all the stock. Leave in the fridge to set for 24 hours.

Veal & apricot terrine

This is a classic style of terrine wrapped in bacon. Pig's liver is fine, but if you have any trimmings from calves' liver, that will go well. Do feel free to experiment with different herbs or seasonings, or pistachios, prunes or sultanas instead of the apricots. It is best to mince the meats for this rather than using a food processor. Ideally, leave to mature for a day or two before eating – it will keep happily for a week or so.

SERVES 8–10

350 g/12 oz lean veal
200 g/7 oz belly pork
200 g/7 oz pig's liver
10 ready-to-eat dried
 apricots, chopped
285 g/10 oz unsmoked
 streaky bacon

MARINADE
8 juniper berries
5 black peppercorns
10 allspice berries
100 ml/3½ fl oz/scant
 ½ cup Cointreau
2 tsp soft brown sugar
2 tsp sage, finely chopped
2 tsp marjoram, finely
 chopped
3 bay leaves
1 tsp freshly grated nutmeg
salt and black pepper

Mince the veal, pork and liver together and mix with the chopped apricots.

To make the marinade, crush the juniper berries, peppercorns and allspice in a pestle and mortar, then mix with the other marinade ingredients. Combine with the minced meats, cover and leave at cool room temperature for about 4 hours.

Preheat the oven to 160°C/325°F/gas 3. You will need a terrine dish measuring 30 x 10 x 7 cm/12 x 4 x 2¾ in or any dish that holds just over 1 litre/1¾ pint/4 cups. Remove the bay leaves from the marinating mixture and arrange in the terrine. Then line it with bacon, making sure the edges don't overlap but leaving no gaps. Spoon the marinated mixture into the terrine, pushing down to make sure there are no air pockets. Cover the top with bacon. Cover with a lid or foil and place in a deep roasting tin; pour in boiling water to come part-way up the sides of the terrine, then place in the oven for about 1½–2 hours. To test, push a thin skewer into the middle of the terrine and leave for a few seconds, then pull it out: if it is hot to the touch, the terrine is done.

Leave to cool for a while, then place a board on top and weight it to press the terrine until it is cold. Chill overnight in the fridge.

To serve, place the terrine in a bowl of warm water for a minute, then invert a plate on top, turn it over and give it a shake – it will just plop out. Serve with toast and cornichons.

See picture overleaf.

Country terrine

Veal has long been prized as a basis for pâtés and terrines, usually mixed with pork or pork fat. The two meats complement each other. Here is a simple terrine to try.

SERVES 8–10

225 g/8 oz diced veal
225 g/8 oz unsmoked
 streaky bacon
350 g/12 oz chicken livers
2 tsp butter
1 onion, finely chopped
3 garlic cloves, crushed
6 juniper berries
10 peppercorns
125 ml/4 fl oz/^{1}/$_2$ cup dry
 white wine
1 tbsp brandy
1 egg, beaten
55 g/2 oz/1^1/$_4$ cups fresh
 breadcrumbs
2 tsp chopped sage
1 tsp chopped rosemary
^{1}/$_4$ tsp grated nutmeg
^{1}/$_2$ tsp ground mace
salt and pepper

Chop the veal, bacon and chicken livers roughly, using a large sharp knife. Heat the butter in a large frying pan over quite a high heat and cook the meats for a few minutes, stirring frequently. Add the onion and cook until softened. Add the garlic and stir for a few more minutes. Remove from the pan and leave to cool.

Preheat the oven to 180°C/350°F/gas 4. Mince the cooled meat mixture or chop in a food processor, but not too finely. Mix in the juniper berries, peppercorns, wine, brandy, egg, breadcrumbs, herbs and spices. When thoroughly mixed, check for seasoning by frying 1 tsp of the mixture in a little butter: taste and adjust the seasoning – it should be well seasoned. Press the mixture into a 1 litre/1¾ pint/4 cup terrine, earthenware dish or loaf tin. Cover with a lid or foil and cook for 1½ hours. To test, push a thin skewer into the middle of the terrine and leave for a few seconds, then pull it out: if it is hot to the touch, the terrine is done.

Leave to cool, then chill overnight in the fridge. The terrine will keep for up to a week. To serve, either scoop it out of the dish or turn out, slice and serve with salad, cornichons and toasted sourdough bread.

Veal stock

Stock is essential to a working kitchen. Without it, sauces will be insipid and lack depth and body. Veal stock is the most versatile: it is used not only for veal and beef dishes, but also for pork and chicken. If you are making stock for a beef dish, you can use beef bones, but never use beef bones for a veal dish because the flavour will be too strong.

Ask your butcher to save some bones for you; you will also need to ask him to chop them up into pieces, to allow maximum flavour to come out. Once you start making your own stock, you will learn to keep vegetable trimmings such as onion ends and celery bases ready for the stock pot.

MAKES ABOUT 1 LITRE/1¾ PINTS/4 CUPS

1 kg/2¼ lb veal bones, chopped
500 g/1 lb 2 oz meat trimmings
2 carrots, roughly chopped
1 onion, roughly chopped
2 celery stalks, roughly chopped
100 ml/3½ fl oz/scant ½ cup dry white wine
2 fresh tomatoes, halved and deseeded
1 tbsp tomato purée
1 garlic clove, crushed
bouquet garni
other herb stalks such as tarragon

Preheat the oven to 230°C/450°F/gas 8. Put the bones and meat trimmings in a roasting pan and brown in the oven for about 15 minutes, turning occasionally to ensure even colouring. Add the carrots, onion and celery to the roasting pan and cook for another 5 minutes or so.

Transfer the bones, meat trimmings and vegetables to a large pan or stock pot, pour in the white wine and allow it to evaporate over a medium heat.

Pour a little water into the roasting pan and over a low heat scrape up any bits; tip these into the stock pot. Add cold water to cover the bones and bring slowly to the boil, but don't allow it to boil hard, otherwise the fat will combine with the stock and create a cloudy stock rather than the clear one we are looking for. Reduce to a gentle simmer, skim off the froth and fat, then add the tomatoes, tomato purée, garlic, bouquet garni and other herb stalks. Simmer for 3–4 hours, skimming occasionally.

Strain the liquid into a bowl and leave to cool. Chill in the fridge; the fat will solidify and can be easily removed.

Stock can be frozen but will keep happily in a covered container in the fridge for up to 5 days.

Reduced stock

This produces a flavoursome stock, ideal for beef dishes, stews, and to make sauces for steaks.

MAKES ABOUT 500 ML/18 FL OZ/2 CUPS

1 onion
1 carrot
1 celery stalk
leek trimmings
6 button mushrooms
2 tsp dripping
2 garlic cloves, crushed
1 tsp tomato purée
100 ml/3½ fl oz/scant ½ cup red wine
1 litre/1¾ pints/4 cups veal stock

Chop all the vegetables into 5 mm/¼ in dice. Heat the dripping in a pan over a medium heat and brown the vegetables in the fat; this may take up to 20 minutes, but it is important to create a lovely brown colour.

Add the garlic and stir for a few minutes. Add the tomato purée and then the red wine, reduce to evaporate and then add the stock, bring slowly to the boil and skim. Leave to simmer gently and reduce by half; this may take about 1 hour. Strain into a clean bowl.

Brine

This salt cure can be used for many types of meat: I often use it for ox tongue (see page 178), and also for pork belly and breast of veal.

2 litres/3½ pints/2 quarts cold water
300 g/11 oz/generous 1 cup coarse sea salt
200 g/7 oz/1 cup coarse brown or granulated sugar
2 bay leaves
3 juniper berries
½ tsp saltpetre (optional)

Put all the ingredients into a large pan and bring to the boil, stirring to dissolve the salt and sugar, then leave until completely cold.

Whichever meat you are using, put it in a deep, non-reactive bowl and pour over the cold brine. Leave for at least 2 days, or up to 7 days.

Saltpetre (potassium nitrate) is a naturally occurring salt that has been used in cured meats since at least the seventeenth century, when it was found to improve the keeping quality of the meat, as well as preserving a deep red-pink colour and adding a slightly piquant flavour. It is now very rarely used in commercial cured meat, and is unnecessary if you are curing meat at home.

Tomato salsa

A refreshing side dish to serve
with chilli con carne, burgers and
barbecues.

SERVES 4

450 g/1 lb ripe tomatoes, blanched, peeled, de-seeded
  and diced, reserving any juice
2 garlic cloves, crushed
1 fresh chilli, de-seeded and finely diced
1 tbsp chopped fresh coriander (cilantro)
6 tbsp olive oil
2 tbsp red or white wine vinegar
salt and pepper

Combine the tomatoes and juice with the garlic,
chilli and coriander. Whisk together the oil and
vinegar, combine with the tomato mixture and
season to taste.

Salsa verde

A punchy little sauce for cold meats,
tongue, veal chops or barbecues.

SERVES 4

2 garlic cloves, crushed
8 canned anchovy fillets
2 tbsp chopped fresh parsley
2 tbsp chopped capers in vinegar
6 tbsp olive oil or rapeseed (canola) oil
pepper

Using a large fork, mash the garlic and
anchovies together, then add the parsley and
capers and 1 tsp of the liquid from the caper jar.
While whisking with the fork, pour in the oil in
a steady stream. Season with pepper to taste –
you probably won't need salt because the
anchovies are salty.

Super-creamy mashed potatoes

Impossible to be precise, because potatoes are all so different. It's not just the variety, but also the soil they grow in that give potatoes their different characteristics. The Desiree potato favoured by Delia Smith grows well in East Anglia, but it can be watery when grown north of the border. My all-time favourite mashing potato is Arran Victory, but it's a shame to peel its glorious purple skin. I've also had good results with Red Duke of York and Maris Piper. Ask for floury or starchy potatoes — technically this means they have a high 'dry matter' content.

SERVES 4

1 kg/2¼ lb good floury
  potatoes
Salt and pepper
250 ml/9 fl oz/1 cup
  full-fat milk
40–70 g/1½ –2½ oz/
  3–5 tbsp butter
Freshly grated nutmeg

Preheat the oven to 150°C/300°F/gas 2. Peel the potatoes and cut into similar-sized pieces, but not too small. Place in a pan, cover with cold water and add 1 teaspoon of salt. Bring to the boil, then simmer gently for 5 minutes.

Drain off all but 1 cm/½ in of water, cover and place in the oven and steam for 30 minutes. When the potatoes are tender and breaking up, drain off any remaining water and place over a low heat, uncovered, shaking the pan from time to time to get rid of all the moisture. Really floury potatoes will break up completely but they will remain beautifully dry, which means they will absorb loads of milk and butter!

Heat the milk with the butter until it melts. Mash the potatoes briefly, adding salt and pepper and a little nutmeg to taste. Add the hot milk and mash in or use a balloon whisk to really get it creamy. Taste to check the seasoning.

RESOURCES

glossary of terms

Bain marie Also known as a water bath or double boiler. A bowl or pan set inside a larger pan; the larger container is filled with hot water to maintain a good temperature without boiling.

Beurre manié Soften an equal amount of butter with plain flour and use to thicken liquids by whisking the resulting paste into them, and then simmering for a few minutes.

Blanch Plunge into boiling water and then refresh in ice cold water until completely cold.

Bouquet garni This is a small bunch of fresh herbs tied with string, used in stews and marinades. Once used, it can be easily discarded. To make, take a square of muslina and place on it a piece of celery about 8 cm/3 in long, a bay leaf, a sprig of thyme, one or two parsley stalks and 6 peppercorns. Fold up the muslin to make a little bag and tie with string so that none of the ingredients can come out. Some people tie the other end of the string to the handle of the pan for ease of finding.

Deglaze Add a splash of liquid, usually wine or other alcohol, to a pan to loosen and dissolve the 'glaze' – the sticky cooking juices at the bottom of the pan. The resulting liquid forms the basis of the sauce.

Degreasing stock The best way is first to allow the stock to cool. Next refrigerate it, and then you will be able to lift off the fat.

Egg wash An egg beaten with a little milk or water and brushed over pastry to give a shiny golden finish.

How to pulp garlic Peel the clove of garlic and place on the corner of a chopping board, sprinkle a small amount of salt over it and, using the back of a large knife, crush the garlic to break it up. Then, using the edge of the knife, pulverise the garlic with the salt. The salt helps to break down the garlic and creates a pulp, thus using all of the garlic and wasting none. It's good either to use the edge of your board or to have a board especially for garlic and onions, as the flavour can linger.

Lardons Small strips of bacon; these can be bought or you can cut thick slices of bacon into 2 cm/¾ in lengths.

Lemon zest The skin of a lemon. Use a sharp peeler or grater to remove as little of the white pith as possible.

Quatre épices Is a classic French spice mix for pâté and terrines consisting of 125 g/4½ oz black pepper, 10 g/¼ oz cloves, 35 g/1¼oz nutmeg, 30 g/1 oz ginger. All ingredients are ground and mixed together.

Reduce Boil the liquid to evaporate some of the water; this concentrates the flavour and thickens the liquid.

Seasoned flour Plain flour which has had the addition of salt and pepper, to season meats as they are coated in flour for frying.

Seasoned milk Take the amount of milk you need and add a small peeled onion stuck with a couple of cloves and a bay leaf. Heat until just below boiling, then leave to infuse for 10 minutes, strain and discard the onion and bay leaf.

INDEX

bibliography

Acton, Eliza *Modern Cookery for Private Families* (1845)

Appelbaum, Robert, *Aguecheek's Beef, Belch's Hiccup, and other Gastronomic Interjections* (2006)

Austin, Thomas (ed.) *Two Fifteenth-Century Cookery-Books* (1888)

Ayto, John *The Diner's Dictionary* (1993)

Beeton, Mrs Isabella *Beeton's Book of Household Management* (1861)

Braudel, Fernand *The Structures of Everyday Life: The Limits of the Possible* (1979, trans. Siân Reynolds)

Brears, Peter *Cooking and Dining in Medieval England* (2008)

Briggs, Richard *The English Art of Cookery* (1788)

Castelvetro, Giacomo *The Fruit, Herbs & Vegetables of Italy* (trans. Gillian Riley, 1989)

Contini, Mary *Dear Francesca* (2002)

David, Elizabeth *French Provincial Cooking* (1969)

Davidson, Alan *The Oxford Companion to Food* (2006)

Davidson, Alan & Jane *Dumas on Food* (1978)

Drummond, J C and Wilbraham, A *The Englishman's Food* (1958)

Flower, Barbara & Rosenbaum, Elisabeth (trans.) *Apicius, The Roman Cookery Book* (1958)

Forme of Cury (1390) (ed. Samuel Pegge, 1780)

Glasse, Hannah *The Art of Cookery, made Plain and Easy* (1747)

Harrison, Molly *The Kitchen in History* (1972)

Hartley, Dorothy *Food in England* (1954)

Henderson, Fergus *Nose to Tail Eating* (2004)

Hickman, Peggy *A Jane Austen Household Book* (1977)

Hope, Annette *Londoners' Larder* (1990)

Larousse Gastronomique (1984)

Luard, Elisabeth *European Peasant Cookery* (1986)

Markham, Gervase *The English Housewife* (1615)

Mason, Laura and Brown, Catherine *The Taste of Britain* (2006)

May, Robert *The Accomplisht Cook* (1660)

McGee, Harold *McGee on Food & Cooking* (2004)

McNeill, F. Marian *The Scots Kitchen* (1929)

Misson's *Memoirs and Observations in his Travels over England* (1698, trans. Mr Ozell 1719)

Ménagier de Paris (1393)

Mennell, Stephen *All Manners of Food* (1985)

Norman, Jill (foreword) *Eating for Victory* – reproductions of Second World War Ministry of Food leaflets (2007)

Pepys, Samuel *Diaries*

Pullar, Philippa *Consuming Passions* (1970)

Rosengarten, David (with Joel Dean and Giorgio DeLuca) *The Dean and Deluca Cookbook* (1996)

Rundell, Mrs Maria *A New System of Domestic Cookery* (1806)

Saulnier, Louis (trans. Edouard Brunet) *Le Répertoire de la Cuisine*

Shephard, Sue *Pickled, Potted and Canned* (2000)

Smith, Andrew F. (ed.) *The Oxford Companion to American Food and Drink* (2007)

Tannahill, Reay *Food in History* (1988)

Time-Life *The Good Cook: Beef & Veal* (1978)

Time-Life *The Good Cook: Offal* (1981)

Trow-Smith, Robert *A History of British Livestock Husbandry to 1700* (1957)

Trutter, Marion *Culinaria Spain* (2004)

Willan, Anne *Great Cooks and their Recipes* (1992)

Wilson, C. Anne *Food and Drink in Britain* (1973)

THANKS

Christopher Trotter

The book is dedicated to my wife Caroline, who still loves veal!

Many thanks once again to Anova Books, in particular Katie Deane for her patience and humour. Fiona Holman for saying yes! Maggie Ramsay for her persistence in perfection and her wonderful contributions. Georgina Hewitt for the inspirational design and all the production team.

I had huge support when compiling the recipes and ideas from, in no particular order: Will Docker from Balgove Larder, whose butcher Graeme helped me understand the cuts; Denise Walton from Peelham Farm and Duncan Lyons from Drumachloy Farm who supplied fabulous veal to devise the recipes; David Naylor with whom I enjoyed hours of conversations and playing in the kitchen to hone ideas; Geoffrey Smeddle of the Peat Inn. Carol Wilson for her initial collaboration, Anne Baker from the United States for an American perspective, and many others in the culinary world and the Guild of Food Writers of which I feel privileged to be a member. Let's make veal more than just a dairy farm by-product!

Maggie Ramsay

Heartfelt thanks to Andrew Fyvie, Helen Roylance, John Gingell, Barbara Mather and Monica and Jim Ramsay for their support and encouragement – and beefeating beyond the call of duty. And the dynamic duo at Anova, Katie Deane and Georgie Hewitt, without whom this book would not be.

I would also like to thank the always helpful and knowledgeable staff of H G Walter, the butcher's shop in Barons Court, London W14. Alternative Meats, a meat-lover's online wonderland, were extremely helpful and sent some exciting boxes of bits. Arlene McKenzie of Nethergate Larder, Ayrshire, Scotland provided fascinating insights into rare-breed meat.

Last but not least

We would also like to thank Andrew and Jo West from Warren Hill Farms who opened their gates and let us take photographs of their wonderful cows.

First published in Great Britain in 2013 by
Pavilion Books
Old West London Magistrates Court
10 Southcombe Street
London, W14 0RA

An imprint of the Anova Books Company Ltd
www.anovabooks.com

Design and layout © Anova Books, 2013
Recipes © Christopher Trotter, 2013
Text © Maggie Ramsay, 2013
Photography © Anova Books except images listed
below in picture credits

Publisher: Fiona Holman
Designer: Georgina Hewitt
Production Manager: Laura Brodie
Commissioning Editor: Katie Deane
Copy Editor and Recipe Tester: Maggie Ramsay
Proofreader: Caroline Curtis
Indexer: Hilary Bird
Photography: Lisa Linder
Illustrator: Alice Lickens
Home Economist: Aya Nishimura
Stylist: Wei Tang

ISBN 978-1-862059894

A CIP catalogue record for this book is available from
the British Library.

10 9 8 7 6 5 4 3 2 1

Reproduction by Mission, Hong Kong
Printed by 1010 Printing International Ltd, China

The moral right of the authors has been asserted.

Picture credits
pg 14: © Universal History Archive/UIG/The
Bridgeman Art Library
pg 19: © J.P. Zenobel/The Bridgeman Art Library
pg 20: © Giraudon/The Bridgeman Art Library
pg 39: © The Art Archive / CCI
pg 206: © Alinari/The Bridgeman Art Library
pg 210: © Archives Charmet/The Bridgeman Art
Library

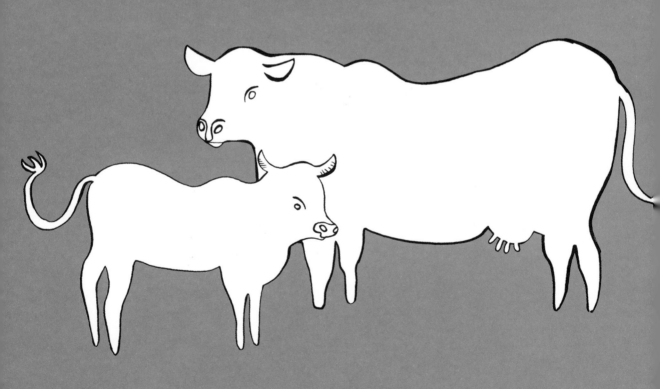